THE EVERYTHING® LARGE-PRINT TRAVEL WORD SEARCH BOOK

Dear Reader,

I think this book can be the perfect travel companion. These word search puzzles are always there for you, and they never complain or talk back! Sure, at times they can be challenging, but with enough dedication, all the words can be found. And in the process, your brain will light up with word-searching joy. What a nice way to pass the time as you fly to an exotic destination or just commute to work.

I've given each word search puzzle a fun travel-related theme. These themes cover the places we travel to, how we get to those places, and what we do once we arrive. We've printed this book with large letters to make the solving less tedious. Your word-finding abilities will be tested, not your vision. So I hope you'll take this book with you on your next journey; I promise it will be a delightful companion!

Charles Timmerman

Welcome to the EVERYTHING® Series!

These handy, accessible books give you all you need to tackle a difficult project, gain a new hobby, comprehend a fascinating topic, prepare for an exam, or even brush up on something you learned back in school but have since forgotten.

You can choose to read an Everything® book from cover to cover or just pick out the information you want from our four useful boxes: e-questions, e-facts, e-alerts, and e-ssentials. We give you everything you need to know on the subject, but throw in a lot of fun stuff along the way, too.

We now have more than 400 Everything® books in print, spanning such wide-ranging categories as weddings, pregnancy, cooking, music instruction, foreign language, crafts, pets, New Age, and so much more. When you're done reading them all, you can finally say you know Everything®!

PUBLISHER Karen Cooper

DIRECTOR OF ACQUISITIONS AND INNOVATION Paula Munier

MANAGING EDITOR, EVERYTHING® SERIES Lisa Laing

COPY CHIEF Casey Ebert

ACQUISITIONS EDITOR Lisa Laing

EDITORIAL ASSISTANT Ross Weisman

EVERYTHING® SERIES COVER DESIGNER Erin Alexander

LAYOUT DESIGNERS Colleen Cunningham, Elisabeth Lariviere, Ashley Vierra, Denise Wallace

Visit the entire Everything® series at *www.everything.com*

THE
EVERYTHING®
LARGE-PRINT
TRAVEL
WORD SEARCH
BOOK

Find your way through 150 easy-to-read puzzles

Charles Timmerman
Founder of Funster.com

Adams Media
New York   London   Toronto   Sydney   New Delhi

Adams Media
An Imprint of Simon & Schuster, Inc.
100 Technology Center Drive
Stoughton, MA 02072

An Everything® Series Book.
Everything® and everything.com® are registered trademarks of Simon & Schuster, Inc.

ADAMS MEDIA and colophon are trademarks of Simon and Schuster.

For information about special discounts for bulk purchases, please contact Simon & Schuster Special Sales at 1-866-506-1949 or business@simonandschuster.com.

The Simon & Schuster Speakers Bureau can bring authors to your live event. For more information or to book an event contact the Simon & Schuster Speakers Bureau at 1-866-248-3049 or visit our website at www.simonspeakers.com.

Manufactured in the United States of America

16 2022

Library of Congress Cataloging-in-Publication Data has been applied for.

ISBN 978-1-4405-2736-4
ISBN 978-1-4405-2739-5 (ebook)

Dedicated to
Suzanne, Calla, & Meryl

Acknowledgments

I would like to thank each and every one of the more than half a million people who have visited my website, *www.funster.com*, to play word games and puzzles. You have shown me how much fun puzzles can be and how addictive they can become!

It is a pleasure to acknowledge the folks at Adams Media who made this book possible. I particularly want to thank my editor, Lisa Laing, for so skillfully managing the many projects we have worked on together.

Contents

Contents

Introduction

The puzzles in this book are in the traditional word search format. Words in the list are hidden in the grid in any direction: up, down, forward, backward, or diagonally. The words are always found in a straight line, and letters are never skipped. Words can overlap. For example, the letters at the end of the word "MAST" could be used as the start of the word "STERN." Only the letters A to Z are used, and any spaces in an entry are removed. For example, "TROPICAL FISH" would be found in the grid as "TROPICALFISH." Apostrophes and hyphens are also omitted in the grids. Draw a circle around each word that you find in the grid. Then cross the word off the list so that you will always know what words remain to be found.

A favorite strategy is to look for the first letter in a word, then see if the second letter is in any of the eight neighboring letters, and so on until the word is found. Or, instead of searching for the first letter in a word, it is sometimes easier to look for letters that stand out, like Q, U, X, and Z. Double letters in a word will also stand out and be easier to find in the grid. Another strategy is to simply scan each row, column, and diagonal looking for any words.

Puzzles

ACTIVITY

ADVENTURE

BAR

BOARDING

CHAIRLIFT

COUNTRY

EQUIPMENT

GONDOLA

GUESTS

HAT

HILLS

HOTELS

ICE

LIFTS

LODGING

MOUNTAIN

PASS

RESORT

RESTAURANT

RUNS

SKI AREA

SKI LIFT

SKI PATROL

SKIERS

SKIING

SLEDDING

SLOPES

SNOWBOARD

SPORT

TOURIST

TRAILS

TRAVEL

VACATION

VAIL

VILLAGE

WINTER

```
T I C E N J V T C L O W L I
R E T N I W H S R E I K S C
A E R A I K S K I L I F T S
V V A C A T I O N U R R S L
E C G T N E M P I U Q E E O
L G N I D R A O B J M S U P
P N I V I L L A G E O T G E
A I G I R E S O R T U A R S
S D D T A H T S F S N U G N
S D O Y I S K I P A T R O L
L E L L I I L O X N A A N I
I L L R I R R S E B I N D F
A S U N I T N V S S N T O T
R O G A M U D V H O T E L S
T C H D R A O B W O N S A F
S C O U N T R Y L I A V L B
```

Solution on Page 304

BANK
CHANNEL
CONGO
DANUBE
DEEP
ELBE
EROSION
FLOWING
GANGES
GULLY
HUDSON
JORDAN
LEVEE
LOIRE
MOUTH
MURRAY
NIGER
NILE
OHIO
ORINOCO
OTTAWA
PATH

POTOMAC
RAFT
RAPIDS
RHINE
SANDBAR
SEINE
SHALLOW
SHORE
SOURCE
STREAM
THAMES
TIBER
TIGRIS
URAL
VOLGA
WATERWAY
YANGTZE
ZAMBEZI

Solution on Page

```
D A Z I M X T T I B E R E K
O T T A W A S D I P A R B F
H T U O M W E H E G U L L Y
P S A N D B A R A E R Z E P
R O T H S Y E T T L P I Z C
N N T H G F A Z E S L R S H
H A O O A H L N I R E O J D
P R H E M M N O G J W I W V
E I U V J A E I W T B A N K
L H D D H M C S L I Z V Y E
I V S C A J U O E P N E S R
N O O C O N I R O G O G H A
Y L N R I R U E R G N I M F
O G D G E C D B X A N A H T
R A E S O U R C E E Y O G O
N R Q C E E V E L A R U C N
```

Solution on Page 304

AXLES

BALANCE

BASKET

BELL

BMX

BRAKES

CHAINS

COMMUTE

CRUISER

CYCLING

FAST

FITNESS

FRAME

FUN

GEARING

HEALTH

HELMETS

LOCK

MIRROR

OIL

PATCH

PEDALS

PUMP

RACING

RIDING

ROAD

SADDLE

SAFETY

SEAT

SPEEDS

SPORTS

STEERING

STREET

TANDEM

TIRES

TOURING

TRICYCLE

UNICYCLE

VEHICLE

WHEELS

```
L Q T L L Q A A Y M Y P X S
S T E E R I N G H T G T V P
D E L L E B F I T N E S S E
P E C W C C U R I E S F B E
E R Y W H Y H L A E K A A D
D T C A L E C T R M L S L S
A S I V O Y E I L A E T A Q
L N R E C X T L N A N S R B
S P T H K M P C S U E E O F
T G N I R A E G F K S H R P
R N E C S E A T A I P S R A
O I O L G N I R U O T R I T
P C D E D X B R P M U P M C
S A A I M D C S T E M L E H
P R O B N T A D E M O I N
L Y R D M G T S E L X A C O
```

AIRPORT	PACIFIC
ALA MOANA	POLYNESIAN
ALOHA	RESORT
AMERICAN	SAND
BAY	STATE
BEACH	SUNSHINE
BUSINESS	TOURISTS
CAPITAL	TRAVEL
CITY	TRIP
CLIMATE	TROPICAL
COCONUT	UNIVERSITY
COUNTY	URBAN AREA
CULTURE	VENUES
HAWAIIAN	WAIKIKI
HISTORY	WATER
HOTELS	
ISLANDS	
LARGE	
LEI	
MOUNTAINS	
OAHU	
OCEAN	

Honolulu

```
W C I T Y A B I L A S C G L
A N W Y R S D N A L S I J G
T N A T O H A F C O E A S L
E R I I T O E T I H N O T P
R E K S S T R I P A I C A A
L K I R I E A M O Y S E T C
M R K E H L N M R T U A E I
I O I V M S A Y T N B N N F
T T U I E L B H L U Y A I I
R R O N A N R C E O U I H C
A O O U T U U A L C P I S U
V P A S R A M E R I C A N L
E R K H E I I B S Z M W U T
L I W N U R S N B D N A S U
L A T I P A C T S L B H T R
T U N O C O C T S L A R G E
```

Solution on Page 304

ABAFT	HELM
ABEAM	HULL
ABOARD	JIB
ADRIFT	KEEL
AFLOAT	KNOTS
AHOY	LEEWARD
ANCHOR	MAST
BATTEN	MATE
BEACON	OCEAN
BERTH	PORT
BILGE	RIGGING
BOAT	RUDDER
BRIDGE	SAILS
BUOY	SEA
CABIN	SHIP
COMPASS	STERN
CREW	WHEEL
DOCK	YAW
FORE	
GALLEY	
GANGWAY	
HARBOR	

Nautically Speaking

```
A N I B A C W W G W I T T F
H T D S B K T H A S A Q O R
W T F L O C N S E Y N R D R
D Y H I A O F O A E E U K Q
C B P A R D D W T M L D H J
X U S S D D G T W S E D H W
D O P S R N A O E H N E P S
B Y O H A B J A R O B R A H
B A R G W P G T C T F A B A
O I T N E Z M A N C H O R N
A R L I E V E O L H G E I G
T Q K G L B O L C L T H D L
U R E G E E C F L A E R G J
K I V I A B E A M L Y Y E I
S T E R N A A K M G U A A B
V K V D H L N P K G S H I P
```

Solution on Page 305

BAROMETER

BLIZZARD

CLIMATE

CLOUDY

COLD

CONDITIONS

COOL

CYCLONE

DROUGHT

DUST

FLOOD

FORECASTS

HAIL

HEAT WAVE

HOT

HUMIDITY

HURRICANES

ICE

JET STREAM

LIGHTNING

LOW

NATURE

NEWS

PREDICTIONS

PRESSURE

RAINFALL

SKY

SNOW

STATION

STORMS

SUNSHINE

TEMPERATURE

TORNADO

TROPICS

TROPOSPHERE

WARM

WET

WINTER

ZONE

Travel Forecast

```
E S C I P O R T H D B Y K S
E U M R A I N F A L L T N N
E N W R C O N D I T I O N S
R S O E O A N Z L S W H C N
U H F Z T T Z T T E U E X O
S I O U X A S A T R R J J I
S N R E R U T A R E P M E T
E E E D D I M I H E D C T C
R H C G O I C P V R Y L S I
P U A N L A S A O C O O T D
R M S C N O W U L O W U R E
E I T E P T G O C D T D E R
T D S O A H N E W S O Y A P
N I R E T E M O R A B O M I
I T H L I G H T N I N G L S
W Y W A R M T O R N A D O F
```

Solution on Page 305

BATHROOM

BELLHOP

BREAKFAST

BUILDING

CHAIN

CLERK

CONCIERGE

EXCLUSIVE

FLOOR

FUN

GIFT SHOP

GUESTS

HILTON

INN

KEY

KING

LARGE

LODGING

LUXURY

MANAGEMENT

MARRIOTT

MOTEL

RATES

RESORT

RESTAURANT

ROOMS

SERVICE

SLEEP

SPA

STAY

SUITES

TALL

TELEVISION

TEMPORARY

TIP

TOURIST

TRAVEL

TRIP

VACATION

VIEW

Staying at a Hotel

```
Y T F D R O O M S L E E P Q
U R M K B R E A K F A S T Y
I O A D I S I N N T L R P U
R S B R E N I A L N D O G A
A E U T O A G G E O Z L O E
T R I T H P V E V I L E N R
E U L C L I M M A S U T V B
S I D V E L H E R I X O A E
H T I W G T A N T V U M C L
Q T N A R U A T S E R O A L
Y O G U E S T S U L Y O T H
E I E C I V R E S E Q R I O
K R E L C L G I F T S H O P
T R I P N T S I R U O T N I
H A K L O D G I N G N A A T
V M E X C L U S I V E B S Y
```

Solution on Page 305

ARMY

BALLOON

BICYCLE

BLIMP

BOAT

BRIDGES

BUS

CABLE

CAMEL

CANAL

CARGO

DIESEL

DRIVING

ENGINE

FERRY

FUEL

GAS

GOODS

HORSE

HUMAN

HYBRID

LAND

LOAD

MODES

MOVING

NAVY

PLANE

PRIVATE

PUBLIC

ROCKET

ROUTES

SEA

SHUTTLE

SPACE

SUBWAY

SYSTEM

TRACTOR

TRAVEL

TRUCK

VAN

Transport

```
B S P A C E F D N A L O A D
G G Y U N S R T R A V E L F
N A V S J M A M N O B L W E
A S A G T O Y A Y P U G A R
S G N B G E C T R A C T O R
T R N R N G M I N S W C E Y
E J A I S L V X H A P B Q S
J C G D V A X U D U M P U V
M N O G T I T I B P I U Q S
E O K E E T R L G L L L H C
G I D S L B I D L A B D R A
E B R E Y C T Q G N I V O M
Z O S H S R Y O A E A T C E
H A M E U R A C S U B S K L
F T V C A B L E I V F U E L
N J K N O O L L A B P E T K
```

Solution on Page 305

AFRICA

ALEXANDRIA

ASWAN DAM

BASIN

BLUE NILE

BOATS

CAIRO

CROSSING

CRUISE

DELTA

DESERT

DRAINAGE

ETHIOPIA

FLOODING

GEOGRAPHY

HEADWATERS

HISTORY

HUGE

HYDROLOGY

IRRIGATION

KHARTOUM

LUXOR

NAVIGATION

NORTH

PHARAOH

PYRAMIDS

RIVERS

RWANDA

SAHARA

SUDAN

TANZANIA

TRAVEL

UGANDA

WHITE NILE

```
A M A D N A W S A Y I H S P
N U L E V A R T A F R I C A
T O E W A N A D U S Y S R D
R T X S H O M V R H B T U N
E R A T O I Z E P S L O I A
S A N A N T T A R L U R S W
E H D O Y A R E U S E Y E R
D K R B W G V X N D N H M W
K R I D O I O I A I I U P C
S D A E R R F L G M L G H R
A E G I X R U R O A E E A O
H L X G N I S A B R T G R S
A T A N Z A N I A Y D I A S
R A A D N A G U E P A Y O I
A I P O I H T E X C D M H N
Z N O R T H F L O O D I N G
```

Solution on Page 306

AIR FORCE

ASPEN

AVALANCHE

BEER

BOULDER

BRONCOS

CANYONS

CATTLE

COLD

COORS

DENVER

FORESTS

GOLD

HISTORY

LANDSCAPE

MESAS

MILE HIGH

MINING

MOUNTAINS

NUGGETS

PIKES PEAK

PLAINS

PUEBLO

RESORTS

RIVERS

ROCKIES

SCENIC

SETTLERS

SKI

SNOW

TOURIST

VACATION

VAIL

WEATHER

WESTERN

WILDERNESS

WILDLIFE

Come to Colorado

```
P  I  K  E  S  P  E  A  K  N  E  P  S  A
U  H  E  Z  C  S  N  I  A  T  N  U  O  M
E  N  V  L  B  R  E  D  L  U  O  B  H  T
B  R  F  S  T  E  O  N  L  J  Y  S  G  S
L  E  S  V  E  T  E  F  R  O  K  N  I  I
O  T  P  O  A  T  A  R  R  E  C  I  H  R
F  S  H  A  C  C  T  C  E  I  D  A  E  U
M  E  E  H  C  N  A  L  A  V  A  L  L  O
I  W  U  P  E  S  O  T  E  N  N  P  I  T
N  S  R  O  O  C  D  R  I  R  Y  E  M  W
I  S  T  E  G  G  U  N  B  O  S  O  D  S
N  H  I  S  T  O  R  Y  A  L  N  K  N  A
G  O  L  D  E  F  I  L  D  L  I  W  I  S
W  O  N  S  T  R  O  S  E  R  H  A  H  E
S  R  E  V  I  R  O  C  K  I  E  S  V  M
R  E  H  T  A  E  W  F  C  I  N  E  C  S
```

Solution on Page 306

AMERICAN

ATLANTIC

BRITISH

CAPE COD

CHURCHES

COLONIST

CORNUCOPIA

DISEASE

ENGLAND

ENGLISH

FEAST

FISHING

FREEDOM

HATS

HISTORY

INDIAN

JAMESTOWN

MAIZE

MAYFLOWER

NATIVE

OCEAN

OLD

PILGRIMS

PROTESTANT

PURITANS

RELIGIOUS

SCURVY

SEPARATIST

SETTLEMENT

SHIP

SICKNESS

SQUANTO

TRAVEL

TURKEY

VOYAGE

Pilgrim's Journey

```
C H U R C H E S C U R V Y T
A H I S T O R Y Z A T T T K
P E R E L I G I O U S N S S
E N G L A N D E Z I A M I I
C G T N E M E L T T E S N C
O L O C E A N A S C F T O K
D I N A C I R E M A N A L N
S S U O N A T I V E W H O E
A H A I P O C U N R O C C S
B F I E R I P U R I T A N S
V R S P I L G R I M S T A T
O E I M A Y F L O W E R I U
Y E O T N A U Q S D M A D R
A D L C I T N A L T A V N K
G O D D I S E A S E J E I E
E M P F I S H I N G J L X Y
```

Solution on Page 306

AIRBOAT

BARGE

BASS BOAT

CANOE

CARAVEL

CATAMARAN

DHOW

DINGHY

DORY

FERRY

FREIGHTER

GONDOLA

HOUSEBOAT

JUNK

KAYAK

KETCH

LIFEBOAT

MOTORBOAT

OUTRIGGER

PADDLE

PONTOON

POWER

PUNT

RAFT

REED BOAT

RIVERBOAT

ROWBOAT

SAILBOAT

SCHOONER

SKI BOAT

SLOOP

STEAMBOAT

SUBMARINE

TRAWLER

TRIMARAN

TUGBOAT

U-BOAT

All Kinds of Boats

```
T U G B O A T R O W B O A T
E R O R T T A O B E F I L R
L E N I R A M B U S R C Z A
D N D V A O O I U B O A T W
D O O E F B N B O P U N T L
A O L R T S Y A R G J O R E
P H A B T S T T R O T E T R
O C T O N A R A M A T A C E
N S D A E B O O O H M O H W
T L C T O E D B G B C I M O
O O A D G B L I M Y D T R P
O O R R O I E K K A R E E T
N P A X A R G S N A E R E K
X B V S F S Y B U U Y T E R
P R E G G I R T U O J A S F
Z I L W O H D I N G H Y K Q
```

Solution on Page 306

ALPS

ALTITUDE

ANDES

ANIMALS

BLUE RIDGE

CLIMATE

CLIMBING

COLORADO

ELEVATION

EROSION

EVEREST

FACE

FOREST

HEIGHTS

HIGH

HIKING

HILL

HIMALAYAS

ICE

LAKES

LANDFORM

NATURE

PEAKS

RANGE

RIVERS

ROCKIES

ROPE

ROUGH

SKIING

SNOW

STEEP

SUMMIT

TALL

TREES

VIEW

VOLCANO

WATERFALL

WEATHER

26

On a Mountain

```
F N S B L P R N E A Q N X O
H I M A L A Y A S L I O K T
J Y C S A U W T D T H I G H
C S I T F S E U G I I T N D
E U S E R Q A R N T K A I W
G M D E E A T E I U I V I E
N M V P T N H H B D N E K I
A I N M A I E G M E G L S V
R T W R W M R U I C E E E O
F P Z O D A R O L O C T I L
I E E F N L O R C S S A K C
G A S D D S P K E E M M C A
A K E N W W E E R O S I O N
Y S K A F O R E S T Y L R O
M T A L L T V O P C E C A F
H I L L H E I G H T S P L A
```

Solution on Page 307

ABIDJAN	OTTAWA
AIRPORTS	PARIS
ATHENS	RIO
ATLANTA	ROME
BAGHDAD	SEATTLE
BANGKOK	SEOUL
BEIJING	SHANGHAI
BERLIN	SINGAPORE
BOSTON	STOCKHOLM
BRUSSELS	SYDNEY
BUDAPEST	TOKYO
CAIRO	TORONTO
CHICAGO	TRAFFIC
DUBLIN	TRAVEL
LIMA	URBAN
LONDON	VENICE
MADRID	VIENNA
MIAMI	
MILAN	
MONTREAL	
MOSCOW	
NAIROBI	

Major Cities

```
N  R  M  V  T  B  U  D  A  P  E  S  T  A
L  E  V  A  R  T  G  N  I  J  I  E  B  N
S  E  O  U  L  A  E  R  T  N  O  M  I  N
K  D  U  B  L  I  N  X  G  C  Y  U  M  E
T  I  E  R  O  M  E  A  B  H  K  R  A  I
R  R  T  U  S  L  P  A  O  I  O  B  I  V
A  D  O  S  T  O  A  B  S  C  T  A  M  E
F  A  R  S  R  H  R  I  T  A  H  N  S  N
F  M  O  E  O  K  I  D  O  G  G  N  N  I
I  A  N  L  P  C  S  J  N  O  E  M  O  C
C  B  T  S  R  O  B  A  G  H  D  A  D  E
A  H  O  N  I  T  H  N  T  S  S  P  N  M
I  O  I  R  A  S  E  A  T  T  L  E  O  I
R  N  A  M  I  L  M  O  S  C  O  W  L  L
O  T  T  A  W  A  T  S  Y  D  N  E  Y  A
S  J  K  O  K  G  N  A  B  E  R  L  I  N
```

Solution on Page 307

AMERICAN	OKLAHOMA
CLINTON	OZARKS
COUNTRY	POOR
DELTA	PRESIDENT
DIAMONDS	RELIGIOUS
ECONOMY	RIVER
FARMING	SIOUX
FISHING	SOUTHERN
FORESTS	STATE
FORT SMITH	TENNESSEE
GEOGRAPHY	TEXARKANA
HISTORY	TOURISM
HOT	UNIVERSITY
HUMID	
HUNTING	
INDIANS	
JONESBORO	
MAP	
MIKE BEEBE	
MISSOURI	
MOUNTAINS	
NATURAL	

Visit Arkansas

```
T A F O R E S T S H U M I D
I N T D J N A T U R A L R I
N A E L S O U T H E R N U A
D M R D E S N I A T N U O M
I O Y I I D I E E T A T S O
A H R W V S V T S T S E S N
N A T M P E E U Y B U X I D
S L N I A E R R H G O A M S
O K U K M S S M P N I R N G
G O O E E S I S A I G K O N
N Z C B R E T I R M I A T I
I A X E I N Y R G R L N N H
T R U E C N N U O A E A I S
N K O B A E N O E F R D L I
U S I E N T P T G T O H C F
H I S T O R Y M O N O C E X
```

Solution on Page 307

AIRCRAFT	LIFT
AIRPLANES	NAVIGATION
BALLISTIC	PHYSICS
BALLOON	PILOT
BIRDS	ROCKETS
BLIMP	SAFETY
DIRECT	SKY
DRAG	SOARING
ENGINE	SPACECRAFT
FLYING	SPEED
FORCE	SUPERSONIC
FUEL	TAIL
GLIDERS	TAKEOFF
GLIDING	TRAVEL
GRAVITY	WINGS
HELICOPTER	WRIGHT
HISTORY	
HYPERSONIC	
INSECTS	
JETS	
LANDING	
LAUNCH	

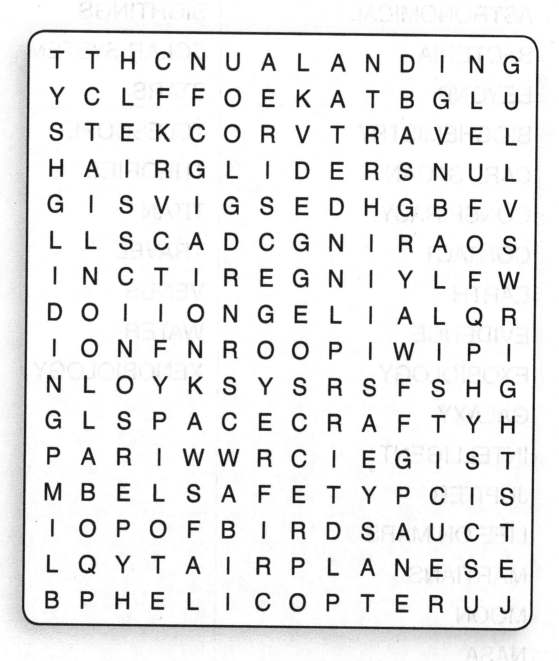

```
T T H C N U A L A N D I N G
Y C L F F O E K A T B G L U
S T E K C O R V T R A V E L
H A I R G L I D E R S N U L
G I S V I G S E D H G B F V
L L S C A D C G N I R A O S
I N C T I R E G N I Y L F W
D O I I O N G E L I A L Q R
I O N F N R O O P I W I P I
N L O Y K S Y S R S F S H G
G L S P A C E C R A F T Y H
P A R I W W R C I E G I S T
M B E L S A F E T Y P C I S
I O P O F B I R D S A U C T
L Q Y T A I R P L A N E S E
B P H E L I C O P T E R U J
```

Solution on Page 307

ADVANCED

ASTRONOMICAL

BACTERIA

BEYOND

BIOCHEMISTRY

CARL SAGAN

CONSPIRACY

CONTACT

EARTH

EVIDENCE

EXOBIOLOGY

GALAXY

INTELLIGENT

JUPITER

LIFE ON MARS

MARTIANS

MOON

NASA

OUTER SPACE

PLANETS

PROBE

SATURN

SETI

SIGHTINGS

SOLAR SYSTEM

STARS

TELESCOPE

THEORIES

TITAN

TRAVEL

VENUS

WATER

XENOBIOLOGY

Alien Travelers

```
L H T R A E C N E D I V E X
O A S M Y G O L O I B O X E
U Y C A R I P S N O C P P N
T C A I R E T C A B M L W O
E N L Q M S N A I T R A M B
R A E I C O N T A C T N E I
S G V G F D N O Y E B E T O
P A A S I E B O R P T T S L
A S R E I L O R R E N S Y O
C L T T W G L N L T A S S G
E R B I O C H E M I S T R Y
S A T U R N S T T A A A A X
U C B P F C A U I N R R L A
S E I R O E H T N N I S O L
W J U P I T E R I E G S S A
T D E C N A V D A T V S I G
```

Solution on Page 308

AIR PUMP

ATTENDANT

CAR WASH

CASHIER

CLERKS

DIESEL

ETHANOL

FILL UP

FLUIDS

FOOD

FUEL

GALLONS

GARAGE

GAS PUMPS

GASOLINE

HIGHWAY

HOSE

MAPS

MECHANIC

MONEY

NOZZLE

OCTANE

OIL

PAY

PETROLEUM

PREMIUM

PRICES

REGULAR

REPAIRS

RESTROOMS

SERVICE

STATION

STORE

TANKS

TIRES

TRAVEL

TRUCK

UNLEADED

VEHICLES

WATER

Filling Stations

```
Y A W H G I H K C U R T J Q
N O I T A T S S R I A P E R
L E V A R T R G A L L O N S
U C A P A Y T A N W A T E R
S L F R G M U E L O R T E P
D E D A E L N U N U Z A S K
I R R S L S A P H D G Z C O
U K E I E S T V M O A E L N
L S U I T R E R C U S N R E
F M F S H H V T O F P E T E
T U I E I S A I V O U R O T
A I L C I N A H C E M E I H
N M L I E M M C J E P S L A
K E U R A E N I L O S A G N
S R P P Y E N O M F O O D O
N P S E R O T S D I E S E L
```

Solution on Page 308

AZTECS

BAJA

BEANS

BORDER

CANCUN

COUNTRY

COZUMEL

CUISINE

CULTURE

FESTIVAL

FIESTA

FOOD

GULF

HISPANIC

HOT

MARIACHI

MAYANS

MEXICANS

MOLE

OAXACA

OLMEC

PESOS

PYRAMIDS

RESORTS

RICE

SHOPPING

SOCCER

SOUTH

SPANISH

TACOS

TAMALES

TEQUILA

TEXAS

TIJUANA

TORTILLA

TOURISM

TRAVEL

TROPICAL

VACATION

YUCATAN

Solution on P

Tour of Mexico

```
M A Z T E C S N A E B A J A
S E L A M A T I J U A N A F
I T Y I X E N I S I U C Z I
R A R E U C S O A X A C A E
U C T O F Q G N I P P O H S
O O N E S E E Z A T F L F T
T S U Z H E S T V C A O G A
S S O C C E R T O C I C O N
K D C I N A P S I H T X A D
H S I N A P S P C V R T E V
X C E M L O O A O E A F S M
W S X L A R I W Z C V L O A
A L L I T R O T U I E U U Y
N U C N A C Y Y M R L G T A
Q I Z M O L E P E S O S H N
B O R D E R U T L U C W S S
```

Solution on Page 308

ADVENTURER

ANTARCTIC

BASE CAMP

BEEKEEPER

BOOTS

BRITISH

CLIMBING

COLD

DISCOVERY

EVEREST

EXPEDITION

EXPLORING

FIRST

HERO

HIGH

HIMALAYAS

HISTORY

ICE

KNIGHTHOOD

MOUNTAINS

NAVIGATOR

NEPAL

NORTH POLE

PEAK

ROPE

SHERPA

SIR

SNOW

SOUTH POLE

SUMMIT

TIBET

TRAVEL

Sir Edmund Hillary

```
S A N T A R C T I C O L D E
A O D P Z U D W R V N I G D
Y R E V O C S I D Q F I A Y
A O X U E L O P H T U O S D
L T P Y S N I A T N U O M C
A A L C K T T C P B D R E L
M G O E N S D U E A I X S I
I I R L I E H S R S P L H M
H V I O G R E P E E K E E B
S A N P H E R H D C R V R I
I N G H T V O I B A O A P N
T E S T H E T S O M P R A G
I P N R O I H T O P E T B F
R A O O O P G O T I M M U S
B L W N D F I R S T I B E T
F R M S J Z H Y K A E P Q P
```

Solution on Page 308

ADDRESS

ART

CARDBOARD

CHEAP

COLLECTOR

DELTIOLOGY

EMBOSSED

ENVELOPE

GREETING

HISTORY

IMAGE

LETTER

MAILING

MESSAGES

NOTES

NOVELTY

OLD

PAPER

PERSONAL

PHOTOGRAPH

PICTURES

PLACE

POSTMARK

QUICK

SCENIC

SENT

SOUVENIR

STAMPS

TOURIST

TRAVEL

VIEW

WRITING

Postcards

```
B Y P P I C T U R E S S Y P
E V U H O T O U R I S T R A
Y G O L O I T L E D S E I P
L E V A R T Y T L E V O N E
K R A M T S O P L E T T E R
M G U Q L W D G D P C U V L
E N V E L O P E R L G T U D
S I N O T E S I A A V S O G
S T R A L S B N O C P L S R
A I Y T O L O Y B E D H P E
G R S B S S E R D D A L A E
E W M P R G P O R T P F E T
S E A E A M S T A M P S H I
E I P M D D K S C E N I C N
N V I M A I L I N G I Y M G
T O U P T Q Q H Q U I C K S
```

Solution on Page 309

ANNUAL	POPULAR
BIKES	RACING
CIRCUITS	RIDERS
CLIMBING	ROADS
CYCLISTS	ROUTE
DISTANCE	SPEED
DOPING	STAGES
ENDURANCE	STEROIDS
EUROPE	STRENGTH
EVENT	SUMMER
FANS	TEAMS
FRANCE	THREE WEEKS
GRAND TOURS	TRAINING
GREG LEMOND	VICTORY
HILLS	WINNERS
JERSEYS	
JULY	
KILOMETERS	
MARATHON	
MILES	
MOUNTAINS	
PEDAL	

Solution on

Tour de France

```
J N A N N U A L G N I C A R
S E G A T S E K I B Z R V O
W Y R O U T E A M S U I I A
S R E T E M O L I K C D C D
U K V S S J S D I O R E T S
M G E V R N E T S M D R O D
M S N E N E I P I N P S R I
E G T I W O J A O U A E Y S
R N Y S N E H M T R C F G T
W I U L I I E T W N U R N A
I P O P U L A R A S U E I N
N O P J G J C R H R L O B C
N D E E P S U Y T T A L M E
E P R P E D A L C T U M I G
R G R A N D T O U R S L L H
S T R E N G T H F R A N C E
```

Solution on Page 309

ARCHITECTURE

ATTRACTIONS

CHICAGO

COUNTRIES

CULTURE

EIFFEL TOWER

EVENTS

EXHIBITIONS

EXPOSITION

FERRIS WHEEL

FUN

HOST CITY

HYDE PARK

INDUSTRY

INNOVATION

INVENTIONS

LARGE

NAO DE CHINA

NEW YORK

PARIS

PEOPLE

PRINCE ALBERT

RIDES

SCIENCE

SPACE NEEDLE

SPECIALIZED

ST. LOUIS

UNIVERSAL

WORLD

```
O E X H I B I T I O N S H K
S K N I N V E N T I O N S R
P U R E X P O S I T I O N O
E L D E E N E C A P S I K Y
C I B A O G A C I H C T R W
I N F U N E R U T L U C A E
A N N F P I C B S I R A P N
L O E L E E H W S I R R E F
I V C A O L I C I Z G T D H
Z A N R P S T N E V E T Y O
E T E G L T E O D D Q A H S
D I I E E I C D W U O S H T
L O C O U N T R I E S A L C
R N S T L O U I S R R T N I
O A K L A S R E V I N U R T
W P R I N C E A L B E R T Y
```

Solution on Page 309

ALPINE

ALTITUDE

ASCENT

ATHLETIC

BELAY

BOOTS

CAMPING

CAVES

COLD

CRAMPONS

DESCENT

EVEREST

EXERCISE

GEAR

GLACIERS

GUIDE

HEIGHTS

HIKING

HILLARY

HIMALAYAS

HOBBY

ICE AXE

MOUNTAINS

NEPAL

OXYGEN

PEAKS

ROCKY

ROPES

SAFETY

SKIING

SNOW

SPORT

STEEP

SUMMITS

TENT

TIBET

TRAINING

TRAVEL

WEATHER

WHITEOUTS

Climb a Mountain

```
Y T E F A S T H G I E H Y Y
S R O C K Y X S O D F E B V
K A W H I T E O U T S N B M
I V E I I V I T S I E U O S
I E A X A M I K C P E U H E
N L T C A T A R A T N B W P
G S H R L E E L R T I E O O
U T E A P X C A A O P L N R
I E R M E S I I T Y L A S N
D N E P T N N S T G A Y U E
E T Q O I S E N N E R S M G
S E O N S R E I C A L G M Y
T B G S E C P O L R G H I X
E I M V S M L L S P O R T O
E T E E A D I Z T N E C S A
P E D C T H I K I N G Y Q E
```

Solution on Page 309

ACADIA

ARCHES

BADLANDS

BEARS

BIG BEND

BISCAYNE

BRYCE

CARLSBAD

COLORADO

DENALI

EVERGLADES

FORESTS

GLACIER

HALEAKALA

HIKING

HISTORIC

LASSEN

MESA VERDE

MOUNTAINS

NATIONAL

OLYMPIC

PARKS

PROTECTED

REDWOOD

RIVER

SAGUARO

SHENANDOAH

TRAIL

VALLEY

WILDERNESS

WILDLIFE

WIND CAVE

YOSEMITE

ZION

Scenic National Parks

```
C C M O U N T A I N S N I Y
I A I D A C A R L S B A D E
R P R O T E C T E D R A S C
O A R C H E S N R L L A H Y
T D K S F V R G L A C I E R
S V A L L E Y S K S I D N B
I R N R D A A D S R L A S
H E O L O G E E M E O D N Y
S D I I U L N V V N L N D O
T W Z A A A O A F A Y E O S
S O R H L D S C N T M B A E
E O R I V E R D I I P G H M
R D W F M S S N R O I I Q I
O E N Y A C S I B N C B Y T
F G N I K I H W P A R K S E
Q E Y Q E F I L D L I W Q B
```

Solution on Page 310

AIDS

BABY DOC

CARIBBEAN

CATHOLIC

CHARITY

CHILDREN

CHOLERA

COFFEE

COLUMBUS

COUNTRY

CREOLE

CULTURE

DISASTER

DISEASE

DOMINICAN

FLOOD

FRENCH

HAITIAN

HELP

HOMELESS

HURRICANE

ISLAND

MALARIA

MANGOES

NATION

OCEAN

PAPA DOC

PLANTAIN

POLITICS

PORT

POVERTY

RED CROSS

REPUBLIC

SOCCER

SUGAR

TROPICAL

WATER

```
S  D  N  A  L  S  I  C  S  D  H  E  L  P
C  S  A  Y  A  R  E  L  O  H  C  N  H  O
I  S  E  O  G  N  A  M  C  U  W  A  C  V
T  O  B  L  E  B  I  H  C  Q  N  I  N  E
I  C  B  S  E  N  A  H  E  W  A  T  E  R
L  E  I  F  I  M  A  B  R  B  C  I  R  T
O  A  R  C  L  R  O  C  Y  D  S  A  F  Y
P  N  A  T  I  O  N  H  I  D  S  H  C  M
T  N  C  T  G  X  O  S  T  R  O  P  I  A
R  C  Y  P  A  P  A  D  O  C  R  C  L  L
O  U  V  D  I  S  E  A  S  E  C  U  O  A
P  L  A  N  T  A  I  N  A  I  D  S  H  R
I  T  W  E  C  H  I  L  D  R  E  N  T  I
C  U  R  C  I  L  B  U  P  E  R  A  A  A
A  R  A  G  U  S  U  B  M  U  L  O  C  S
L  E  E  F  F  O  C  R  E  O  L  E  Q  L
```

Solution on Page 310

ADMISSION

AUTOPIA

CALIFORNIA

CASTLE

CHARACTERS

CHILDREN

CROWDS

DREAM

DUMBO

EARS

FAMILY

FIREWORKS

FOOD

FUN

GOOFY

GUESTS

HOTELS

LINES

MATTERHORN

MEMORIES

MONORAIL

MUSIC

ORIGINAL

PARADES

PRINCESS

RESORT

RIDES

SHOWS

SNOW WHITE

SOUVENIRS

TICKETS

VACATION

Solution on P

Let's Go to Disneyland

```
S U S T E K C I T M U S I C
T H O T E L S Z Y L I M A F
S C U O B M U D E A R S C V
E R V N R O H R E T T A M X
U M E M O R I E S L L R Y L
G O N T T S B A E I E K A X
R N I P C R N M F S J N E P
I O R X T A D O O F I O F C
D R S V P L R R W G B I Z H
E A D A R N T A I W R S J I
S I W C I Y X R H E H S E L
H L O A N P O Q W C F I N D
O I R T C G O O F Y X M T R
W N C I E L R T O U E D Y E
S E Y O S K M U U E N A K N
W S H N S Z P A R A D E S L
```

Solution on Page 310

AUTOMATIC

BATTERY

BMW

BRAKES

BUMPER

CADILLAC

CHEVROLET

CHRYSLER

DIESEL

DRIVER

ELECTRIC

ENGINE

EXHAUST

FUEL

GASOLINE

HENRY FORD

HIGHWAY

HYBRID

INSURANCE

LICENSE

MECHANIC

MOTOR

OIL

PASSENGERS

POLLUTION

ROADS

SEAT BELT

SEDAN

SPEED

SUV

TIRES

TOYOTA

TRAFFIC

TRUNK

VAN

VEHICLE

WHEELS

WINDOWS

WINDSHIELD

```
T Z D I E S E L C I H E V T
C L O I L I C E N S E W Y I
W I E C H R Y S L E R H R R
B I F B T S U A H X E E E E
R W N F T R D E E P S E T S
A E B D A A N S U V L L T N
K C P N S R E G N E S S A P
E H C M Y H T S C A P V B C
S E H F U C I T A M O T U A
W V O I X B R E O S L E A L
O R T R G I M T L E L N T L
D O R E C H O W U D U I O I
N L U V V R W F F A T G Y D
I E N I L O S A G N I N O A
W T K R D I R B Y H O E T C
R O A D S M E C H A N I C I
```

Solution on Page 310

AMTRAK

BOGIES

BOXCAR

CARS

COAL

CONDUCTOR

CONNECT

CROSSING

DEPOT

DIESEL

DINING CAR

DISTANCE

ELECTRIC

ENGINE

EXPRESS

FREIGHT

HIGH SPEED

LIGHT RAIL

LINE

LOCOMOTIVE

LONG

MAGLEV

METRO

MONORAIL

PASSENGERS

PULLMAN

RAILCAR

RAILROADS

RAILWAYS

SCHEDULE

SEATS

STATION

STEAM

TRAVEL

TUNNELS

VEHICLES

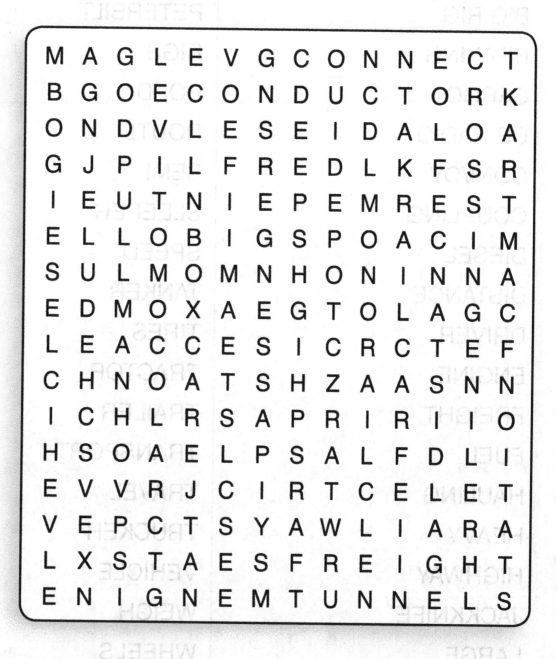

```
M A G L E V G C O N N E C T
B G O E C O N D U C T O R K
O N D V L E S E I D A L O A
G J P I L F R E D L K F S R
I E U T N I E P E M R E S T
E L L O B I G S P O A C I M
S U L M O M N H O N I N N A
E D M O X A E G T O L A G C
L E A C C E S I C R C T E F
C H N O A T S H Z A A S N N
I C H L R S A P R I R I I O
H S O A E L P S A L F D L I
E V V R J C I R T C E L E T
V E P C T S Y A W L I A R A
L X S T A E S F R E I G H T
E N I G N E M T U N N E L S
```

Solution on Page 311

AXLE

BIG RIG

BRAKING

CARGO

CB RADIO

CONVOY

COUPLING

DIESEL

DISTANCE

DRIVER

ENGINE

FREIGHT

FUEL

HAULING

HEAVY

HIGHWAY

JACKKNIFE

LARGE

LICENSE

LIGHTS

LOAD

LONG HAUL

LORRY

PETERBILT

RIGS

ROAD

ROUTE

SEMI

SLEEPER

SPEED

TANKER

TIRES

TRACTOR

TRAILER

TRANSPORT

TRAVEL

TRUCKER

VEHICLE

WEIGH

WHEELS

Semi Trucks

```
L O R R Y S E M I V T R S T
S C W W E I G H E A V Y R I
P A D C T L A R G E A U R R
E R R W H E E L S W C E E E
E G I R G I B S H K P U L S
D O V E I N C G E E K E I P
R T E C E B I R E I U F A E
C O R N R H G L O F D I R T
O G U A F S S N P A H N T E
N N D T N E E G I U D K F R
V I A S E S T N I L O K S B
O K O I L N P A I R U C M I
Y A L D X E L O N G H A U L
F R T R A C T O R K N J H T
K B V E H I C L E T E E Z E
S T H G I L I L E V A R T C
```

Solution on Page 311

ALMONDS

APPLES

BAG

BREAK

CAKE

CANDY BAR

CARROTS

CHEETOS

CHOCOLATE

COOKIES

CORN CHIPS

CRACKERS

DOUGHNUTS

DRINK

FRESH

FRUIT

HEALTHY

ICE CREAM

JERKY

JUNK FOOD

NOODLES

PACKAGED

POPCORN

PORTABLE

PRETZELS

PROCESSED

QUICK

SANDWICH

SATISFYING

SEEDS

SMALL

SNICKERS

SWEET

TRAIL MIX

VEGETABLES

Travel Snack

```
T S E I K O O C V J E R K Y
C T E G A B M A E R C E C I
R O S L Q D O U G H N U T S
A R R W P R O C E S S E D A
C R U N E P S N T E N Y E N
K A P E C E A R A R I H G D
E C C T E H T O B F C T A W
R D P A C H I C L X K L K I
S P O L N D S P E I E A C C
Q S R O K D F O S M R E A H
U D T C F N Y P J L S H P E
I N A O R K I B Z I D B L E
C O B H U M N R A A E C L T
K M L C I F G U D R E A A O
S L E Z T E R P J T S K M S
K A E R B N N O O D L E S G
```

Solution on Page 311

ANCHOR

BALCONY

BEACHES

BEDS

BUFFETS

CABINS

CAPTAIN

CASINO

CREW

DANCING

DINING

DOCK

DRINKING

EXCURSIONS

FUN

GAMBLING

LIFE VEST

LIFEBOAT

LUGGAGE

MEAL

PORTHOLE

READING

RELAXATION

SAILING

SALT AIR

SEA BREEZE

SEASICK

SHOPPING

STERN

SUN TANS

SUNBATHING

SUNSHINE

TOURISTS

TUGBOAT

VACATION

WATER

Pleasure Cruise

```
R S W S U N T A N S K C O D
E T E H N D A N C I N G W I
A S R O R E L A X A T I O N
D I C P E X K C I S A E S I
I R L P T C A P T A I N R N
N U I I S U N B A T H I N G
G O F N C R C A B I N S W X
J T E G K S E A B R E E Z E
B P B G N I L B M A G R B N
E S O E O O N I S A C B A I
A T A R D N E G A G G U L H
C E T L T S E V E F I L C S
H F C A T H V A C A T I O N
E F Y E T A O B G U T G N U
S U U M S A I L I N G F Y S
I B A N C H O R E T A W A H
```

Solution on Page 311

AFRICA

ARABIAN

ARIZONA

ATACAMA

BARREN

BEDOUIN

CACTUS

CALIFORNIA

CLIMATE

COLD

COYOTE

DIURNAL

DROUGHT

DUNES

EGYPT

EXTREME

GOBI

HEAT

HOT DESERTS

HUMID

KALAHARI

LANDSCAPE

LIFE

LIZARDS

MOJAVE

MOUNTAINS

NEVADA

RAINFALL

REGION

SAHARA

SANDSTORM

SCORPIONS

SNAKES

SONORAN

SUN

TEMPERATURE

WATER

WIND

Desert Journey

```
T N E V A D A S E K A N S Y
S A A R I Z O N A R O N O S
S A E I R L A N D S C A P E
K E H H B K I Z H U M I D N
T M N A S A N D S T O R M S
H E A U R L R W L C R M N D
G R M F D A O A I A A O E I
U T A P X H F T Z C I U R U
O X C F E A I E A P N N R R
R E A C R R L R R K F T A N
D E T N O I A O D K A A B A
E T A M I L C T S N L I W L
G O B I X S D A U Y L N I I
Y Y H O T D E S E R T S N F
P O X P B N I U O D E B D E
T C M O J A V E R E G I O N
```

Solution on Page 312

ACCIDENTS

ANGER

BUSES

CARS

CITIES

CONGESTION

DIRECTION

DRIVERS

DRIVING

EXIT

FAST

FREEWAYS

GRIDLOCK

HEAVY

HIGHWAYS

INTERSTATE

JAMS

LANES

LATE

MOVING

NEW YORK

PASSING

PEOPLE

POLICE

RED LIGHTS

ROAD RAGE

ROADWAY

RULES

RUSH HOUR

SIGNS

SLOW

SPEED

STOP SIGN

STREETS

TICKET

TRAVEL

TRUCKS

VEHICLES

```
D K R O A D W A Y E T A L M
R E G N A C C I D E N T S O
U L E C O N G E S T I O N V
L T A P H I G H W A Y S T I
E E S N S T E E R T S T D N
S K V R E J H P A S S I N G
G C C A A S H O H R R S S I
N I S O R C T I X E T R V R
I T N M L T I H C T A E V E
V T G S A D F T G N H V C N
I R I Y L J I B I I Y I Y E
R U S H H O U R C E L R D W
D C P E N S W L G O S D Q Y
K K O X E P E O P L E P E O
W S T S H S E G A R D A O R
H Z S Y A W E E R F A S T K
```

Solution on Page 312

ANCHOR

ARTIFICIAL

BARGES

BOATS

BOSTON

CARGO

CITIES

COAST

DOCK

DREDGING

HARBOR

HAVEN

INLAND

JETTY

LOADING

LONG BEACH

MARINA

NATURAL

NEW YORK

PIER

PORTS

PROTECT

SAN DIEGO

SEA

SHELTER

SHIPS

STORM

TIDE

TRADE

WATER

WAVES

WEATHER

WHARF

```
S R K L C T S A O C R W B P
K R V F A N C H O R B N I F
C B S N R R Y D E O A E V F
K T A T G A U W A L R N Q S
E I S R O S H T M S T R O P
U N P E G R S W A G I E G I
W L R H D E M E R N F L R H
H A O T L A S D I I I H C S
M N T A F G R I N D C H I E
N D E E Y W N T A A I S T A
F O C W R T O I E O A E I N
A T T D Y Z T B G L L V E E
L T K S D O G E I D N A S V
W A U C O N R V J Z E W U A
C B F I O B W K R O B R A H
Y M L L M D U O S Z K W D B
```

APPAREL

BELTS

BLOUSE

BUTTONS

CASUAL

CLOAK

COATS

COTTON

DRESSES

FABRIC

FIT

GLOVES

HATS

HEM

JACKET

JEANS

JUMPER

MODELS

PAJAMAS

PANTS

PONCHO

PURSES

SCARVES

SEWING

SHAWL

SHIRTS

SHORTS

SILK

SIZE

SKIRTS

SLEEVE

SOCKS

STYLE

SWEATER

T SHIRT

TIE

UNIFORM

WARMTH

WOOL

ZIPPER

Clothes to Pack

```
G L Q S W O S J L O O W S P
S W U T O W A R M T H I A L
N A L Y N C A S U A L N U S
N H B L K C K P C K T S T N
R S G E E O T S P S R E N O
E T T B L T J G Z A N S P T
P R I R L T L X X M R S R T
P O N C H O S S R A R E A U
I H M R V N U O C J T R L B
Z S S E T I F S C A G D F Z
F L S P H I N O E P R A S M
D E E M N A A W J U B V L N
Q E W U E T S H I R T S E H
E V I J S I Z E I S I T D S
M E N K A O L C W E E A O W
S H G L S T R I K S F H M D
```

Solution on Page 312

AIR TRAVEL

BEACHES

CALIFORNIA

CHICAGO

CITIES

FAMILIES

FESTIVALS

FLORIDA

FOREIGN

GAMBLING

HAWAII

HIKING

HISTORY

HOTELS

INDUSTRY

LANDMARKS

MONUMENT

MOTEL

MOUNTAINS

MUSEUMS

NEW YORK

ORLANDO

RECREATION

RESORTS

STATES

SUMMER

TOURIST

TRAINS

TRIPS

VACATIONS

WATER

YOSEMITE

Touristy

```
T D H S S F L O R I D A S R
S G I N L N E W Y O R K M H
I P K I A H V R E T A W U I
R T I A V V A B E A C H E S
U S N R I I R W I F N N S T
O N G T T V T N A O S G U O
T O H V S K R M I I N I M R
L I O W E O I T G A I E R Y
J T T H F L A N D M A R K S
C A E I I E I S L E T O M A
H C L E R L T J O F N F K V
I A S C B A Y R T S U D N I
C V E M T N E M U N O M G N
A R A E K C Y O S E M I T E
G G S T R O S E R E M M U S
O R L A N D O S E I T I C W
```

Solution on Page 313

BIKES	PARTS
BRAKES	PASSENGER
CHOPPER	POWER
CHROME	RACING
CRUISING	RIDERS
CYCLE	RIDING
ENGINE	ROAD
FAST	SAFETY
FREEDOM	SCOOTERS
GANGS	SEAT
GRIP	SIDECAR
HARLEY	SPEED
HELMET	SUZUKI
HIGHWAY	TRAFFIC
HONDA	TRAVEL
INDIAN	WHEELIES
JACKET	WIND
KAWASAKI	YAMAHA
LEATHER	
MOPEDS	
MOTORBIKE	
PANNIERS	

Motorcycle Touring

```
D E E P S G A H A M A Y G L
A L B S T R A P J A C K E T
O C X S E I L E E H W V N I
R Y C S S K A W A S A K I K
V C R U I S I N G R S F G U
P V S E K A R B T U E R N Z
P A S S E N G E R R A E E U
S G N A G R S C O O T E R S
U W I N D I A N H H T D T I
O U I H I G H W A Y R O E D
C H O P P E R S R B A M M E
L E A T H E R A L Y F O L C
R E W O P E C S E E F P E A
D G N I D I R R Y S I E H R
Q D R I N E M O R H C D Y T
A G R G F R Y T E F A S T S
```

Solution on Page 313

BOATS

CATAMARAN

CATBOAT

CREW

CRUISING

CUTTER

DINGHY

FLOAT

FORE

FUN

GALLERY

HEADSAIL

HULLS

JIB

KEEL

KETCH

LAKE

MAINSAIL

MASTS

OAR

OCEAN

PORT

RACING

RECREATION

RIG

ROPE

RUDDER

SAILING

SCHOONER

SEA

SHIP

SLOOP

SPEED

SPINNAKER

STERN

VESSEL

WATERCRAFT

WIND

YACHTING

YAWL

```
L P R K S P E E D D T L D O
G O R F Q L B F C H W E C X
O I K E C A O L S L M E L C
N R R E A K A O I H A K R U
U O E H T E T A P N I X G C
F Y I P B C S T E N N P N G
P O R T O D H R A O S V I A
E R T F A R C R E T A W C L
P G E E T E A W D E I D A L
W N H K R M R G S X L I R E
J I B U A E S C H O O N E R
N T N T L N D T E B Y G T Y
K H A D G L N D E R E H T A
Q C L G N I S I U R C Y U W
Q A L E S S E V P R N L C L
T Y T G N I L I A S T S A M
```

Solution on Page 313

AKRON

AMERICAN

AVIATION

BASEBALL

BELLWETHER

BENGALS

CAMBRIDGE

CANTON

CARDINAL

CINCINNATI

COLUMBUS

CORN

DAYTON

FOOTBALL

GOVERNOR

INDIANS

KENT

LAKE ERIE

LOTTERY

OHIO RIVER

OHIO STATE

OHIOANS

PLAINS

POPULATION

PORTSMOUTH

SENECA

TOLEDO

UNIVERSITY

USA

YOUNGSTOWN

The Buckeye State

```
F O O T B A L L S E N E C A
T Z H L E G D I R B M A C V
O B E L L W E T H E R B W I
L N T A A P N A C I R E M A
E O A B N O U N Y E P N D T
D T T E I P L N P I O G X I
O Y S S D U Y I G R R A E O
H A O A R L T C O E T L M N
I D I B A A I N V E S S F L
O C H L C T S I E K M N I O
A A O H N I R C R A O I N T
N N A E N O E O N L U A D T
S T K S I N V R O N T L I E
Z O R H U C I N R T H P A R
G N O Y O U N G S T O W N Y
H Q N C O L U M B U S X S T
```

Solution on Page 313

AMTRAK
BUILD
BUSINESS
CARS
CIVIL WAR
COAL
CONDUCTOR
CONRAIL
DIESEL
ENGINEERS
EXPANSION
FREIGHT
GAUGE
INDUSTRY
IRON
JAY GOULD
LOCOMOTIVE
PACIFIC
PASSENGERS
PULLMAN
RAILROADS
REVOLUTION

SPEED
STATION
STEEL
STRIKES
TECHNOLOGY
TRACKS
TRAINS
TRAVEL
WESTERN

Railroad History

```
Y N O I T U L O V E R E A Q
Z Y K H Q E O D K M K X M L
L E S E I D C S E Z J P T E
T R A C K S O H E E R A R E
T R A I N S M B N A P N A T
Q G W F L A O C W O P S K S
F R E I G H T L L A L I R J
P A N C C T I E S B D O E J
U I G A R V V S U S T N G A
L L I P I A E S T C W L U Y
L R N C R N I A U A E I A G
M O E T G N T D T R S A G O
A A E E I N D U S T R Y U
N D R S O O N O R I E N S L
E S S N C D L I U B R O D D
Y P V S T R I K E S N C H L
```

Solution on Page 314

ACCRA	MADRID
ALGIERS	MANILA
AMMAN	MONACO
ANKARA	MOSCOW
ATHENS	NASSAU
BAGHDAD	OSLO
BANGKOK	OTTAWA
BEIJING	PARIS
BEIRUT	PIERRE
BELFAST	PRAGUE
BERLIN	QUITO
CAIRO	RABAT
CARACAS	ROME
DUBLIN	SEOUL
HANOI	TOKYO
HAVANA	TRIPOLI
HELSINKI	VIENNA
JAKARTA	WARSAW
KIEV	
LIMA	
LISBON	
LONDON	

Capitals Around the World

```
G M A D R I D B S A M M A N
Z R N U U V V I E N N A A H
R O O B S I R A P I E R R E
A M D L Q U I T O T R H Z C
B E N I L R E B H S A U T N
A M O N A C O J A K A R T A
T O L I I P B A N G K O K S
O S U S L R B S O J H K T S
K C O N O A E K I E V D S A
Y O E O P G I V L A H A A U
O W S B I U J S H R C L F D
L A P S R E I G L A L I L A
S S T I T N N A R K V N E R
O R O L K A G A D N J A B C
I A L I M A C R H A V M N C
U W Q C C A I R O T T A W A
```

Solution on Page 314

ADDRESS	NAME
ALLEY	ONE WAY
ASPHALT	PARKING
AVENUE	PASS
BRICK	PAVEMENT
BUILDINGS	PLACE
BUSY	PUBLIC
CARS	ROADS
CHILDREN	SIDEWALKS
CIRCLE	SIGNS
CITY	TAR
CONCRETE	TOWN
CURBS	TRAFFIC
DIRECTION	TRAVEL
DRIVE	TREES
EASEMENT	URBAN
GRAVEL	VEHICLES
HIGHWAYS	VENDOR
LANES	
LIGHTS	
LINES	
MOTORWAYS	

On the Street

```
Y C U R B S O N E W A Y X P
E T C N W O T U H S S A P A
C B I H Q P N H K H P L S V
A C R C I E S L G A H Y E E
L L C I V L A R G I A B N M
P R L A C W D R A W L U A E
U O E E E K A R R C T S L N
T A H D Y V R O E O G Y G T
S D I R E C T I O N N S N R
N S G L A O I R I C A E I A
G E H M M T D D E R M L K F
I N W P U B L I C E E C R F
S I A D R I V E S T S I A I
D L Y F U T R A V E L H P C
X Y S B S S E R D D A E A S
N A B R U H R O D N E V I J
```

Solution on Page 314

BIG MAC

BREAKFAST

CHEESEBURGER

COFFEE

COKE

DOLLAR MENU

EGG MCMUFFIN

FAST FOOD

FISH FILET

FRENCH FRIES

GOLDEN ARCHES

HAMBURGERS

HAPPY MEALS

ICE CREAM

KETCHUP

MCCAFE

MCCHICKEN

MCDOUBLE

MCGRIDDLE

MCRIB

MILKSHAKES

PIES

QUARTER POUNDER

SANDWICHES

SNACK WRAP

SODA

SUNDAES

TASTY

TEA

WRAPS

Stop at McDonald's

```
M C R I B F A S T F O O D S
R H M C G R I D D L E O G P
S E K A H S K L I M L O U A
E E L B U O D C M L L H T R
I S E A D N U S A D C U J W
R E D N U O P R E T R A U Q
F B C O K E M N E Y T S A T
H U O B R E A K F A S T W E
C R F K N R B I G M A C T L
N G F U C H M A E R C E C I
E E E H A P P Y M E A L S F
R R E G G M C M U F F I N H
F S R E G R U B M A H T J S
A D O S E H C I W D N A S I
Y S N A C K W R A P I E S F
N E K C I H C C M C C A F E
```

Solution on Page 314

AIRCRAFT

AIRLINES

AIRPORTS

AIRSPACE

ALTITUDE

APPROACH

ARRIVAL

AVIATION

BROADCAST

CALL SIGN

CLEARANCE

COMPUTERS

CONTACT

CRASH

DEFENSE

DELAYS

DEPARTURE

DIRECTION

FAA

FLIGHTS

FLOW

GROUND

LANDING

LANGUAGE

MILITARY

PILOTS

RUNWAYS

SAFETY

SECURITY

TAKEOFF

TAXI

TECHNOLOGY

TERMINAL

TOWERS

Air Traffic Control

```
T S S X Z T C A T N O C O P
A E T D R C A F P I L O T S
K N R H I F A S R E W O T L
E I O S D R E C A P S R I A
O L P A C T E R M I N A L N
F R R R T S A C D A O R B G
F I I C E N O I T A I V A U
D A A D C A L L S I G N L A
E P S E H R Y D R Y O D A G
F P Y P N R R E E T S N N E
E R A A O I A L T I T U D E
N O W R L V T A U R H O I I
S A N T O A I Y P U G R N X
E C U U G L L S M C I G G A
F H R R Y P I B O E L W Z T
S A F E T Y M N C S F L O W
```

Solution on Page 315

ANACONDA

ANIMALS

ARGENTINA

BEACHES

BOLIVIA

BRAZIL

CHILE

COCAMA

COLOMBIA

CONTINENT

COUNTRY

CUISINE

CULTURE

ECUADOR

GOLD

GUYANA

HISTORY

INCAS

INDIANS

JAGUAR

LANDMASS

LATIN

LIMA

LLAMAS

PARAGUAY

PERU

PIRANHA

QUECHUA

RIO

SAMBA

SPANISH

SURINAME

TOURISM

TRAVEL

TRINIDAD

URUGUAY

VALDIVIA

VENEZUELA

Explore South America

```
E L A T I N O T R A V E L I
R O D A U C E L I H C I L D
U C L B R A Z I L V M C A A
T B O L I V I A A A I G M D
L T G C S S N N R L N S A I
U O C Y A D A A G D D V S N
C U U Y M M L C E I I E P I
O R I A B U A O N V A N A R
U I S U A C O N T I N E N T
N S I G H R Y D I A S Z I A
T M N A I E M A N I R U S U
R H E R S E H C A E B E H H
Y K V A T B A I B M O L O C
U R E P O S L A M I N A I E
A H N A R I P Y A U G U R U
O A N A Y U G R A U G A J Q
```

Solution on Page 315

AIR

BELL

BLACK

BOILER

BUFFERS

CARS

CHASSIS

COAL

CREW

DIESEL

DRIVER

ENGINEER

EXHAUST

FAST

FIREBOX

FREIGHT

FUEL

GEARS

HEAT

HISTORICAL

INVENTION

LOCOMOTIVE

PASSENGER

PISTON

POLLUTION

POWER

PRESSURE

RAILROAD

RAILWAYS

SPEED

STATION

STOKERS

TECHNOLOGY

TENDER

TRAVEL

VALVES

WHEELS

WHISTLES

WOOD

```
T A E H R T H G I E R F D R
T T X O B E R I F U E L E A
L R S S U C E B E L L V E S
O A A A F H I N F C I T P L
C C C V F N N E I R O E S E
O K A I E O V X D G B N L E
M P V R R L E H A O N D Q H
O O A Q S O N A O C S E B W
T L L S V G T U R O R R L L
I L V C S Y I S L A E U A U
V U E H R E O T I L K S C P
E T S A A E N L A H O S K I
D I E S E L W G R N T E D S
O O W S G A K O E I S R Y T
O N I I Y Q T W P R I P E O
W H I S T L E S T A T I O N
```

Solution on Page 315

ALGAE

BAIKAL

BASS

CLEAR

COOL

CRATER

DAM

DEEP

DEPTH

ECOSYSTEM

ERIE

FISH

FLOW

FUN

GLACIAL

GREAT

HURON

ICE

INLAND

LARGE

MICHIGAN

MOSS

MOUNTAIN

NATURAL

ONTARIO

PLANTS

PONDS

RECREATION

RESERVOIR

RIVERS

SALT WATER

SAND

SHORE

SKI

STREAMS

SUMMER

SUPERIOR

TURTLE

VALLEY

WET

```
K D N A L N I J D Q B D Q F
K S A M O U N T A I N A U E
P U T E A G L A M B M R S A
O M U S A N D N G A K G S S
N M R E S E R V O I R L K T
D E A E E Z G T R K H A I R
S R L P C N U E E A M C O E
S H O R E R T G T L E I I A
Z M U I T A E R A E T A R M
F G D L R G I A W D S L A S
S K E C I E R L T C Y T T T
O B P O V A P E L I S F N N
G F T O E E W U A Y O U O A
U A H L R M O S S T C N R L
L F C I S A V A L L E Y U P
R Z E E C H W O L F I S H K
```

Solution on Page 315

AGENT

AIRCRAFT

AIRPLANES

AIRPORT

AMERICAN

ARRIVAL

ATTENDANT

AVIATION

BAGGAGE

BOEING

CABIN

CAPTAIN

CREW

DEPARTURE

ECONOMY

FLIGHT

FREIGHT

FUEL

GATE

JETBLUE

LUGGAGE

NORTHWEST

PASSENGERS

PASSPORT

PILOTS

PRICES

RUNWAY

SAFETY

SCHEDULE

SECURITY

SERVICES

SKY

SOUTHWEST

TERMINAL

TICKETS

US AIRWAYS

```
E U L B T E J Y T E F A S F
C N A G E N T H G I E R F U
R O V V N R G S E C I R P E
E I I Q O I F E G A G G U L
W T R P L R U N W A Y K S A
N A R F A T T E N D A N T N
I I A Y U S A I R W A Y S I
A V Y T W E S D X B E S E M
T A M I A N T E G A L E W R
P M O R I A E P N G U C H E
A E N U R L K A I G D I T T
C R O C C P C R E A E V U A
A I C E R R I T O G H R O G
B C E S A I T U B E C E S Y
I A I K F A T R O P S S A P
N N O R T H W E S T O L I P
```

Solution on Page 316

AUTO

BICYCLE

BMX

BOAT

CAMEL

CYCLING

DERBY

DRAG

FOOT

GREYHOUND

HORSE

KART

MARATHON

MOTOCROSS

MOTORCYCLE

MOTORSPORT

OFF ROAD

OLYMPICS

RALLY

RELAY

ROWING

RUNNING

SAILING

SKATING

SKIING

SLED DOG

SNOWMOBILE

SPEED

SPRINT

STOCK CAR

SWIMMING

TOUR

TRACK

```
S K I I N G A T S P E E D C
W I T T R A C K G P H V B J
I E X X E Y G Y H O R S E J
M D G H C L L N L K A I P M
M F N L N L I Y I M U Q N O
I O I U A Q M B A W T C D T
N N T R O P S R O T O M Y O
G F A O I H A L Y M Y R V C
N O K C R T Y D E A W N L R
I O S Z H C Y E L D U O A O
N T A O B B Y E R Q D C N S
N R N M R D R C B G K O M S
U A X E C A M E L C A E G A
R K D A O R F F O E V R S P
C K V B R U O T B I R X D V
G N I L I A S B I C Y C L E
```

Solution on Page 316

ACTIVITIES

ADMISSION

ANCIENT

ANTIQUE

ARTIFACTS

ARTISTIC

CASES

CHILDREN

COLLECTION

CULTURE

CURATOR

DINOSAURS

DISPLAYS

EDUCATION

EXHIBITS

FAMOUS

GALLERY

HISTORICAL

LEARNING

MODERN

NATURAL

OBJECTS

OLD

PAINTINGS

PUBLIC

RARE

SCIENTIFIC

SCULPTURES

TOURS

TREASURES

VISITORS

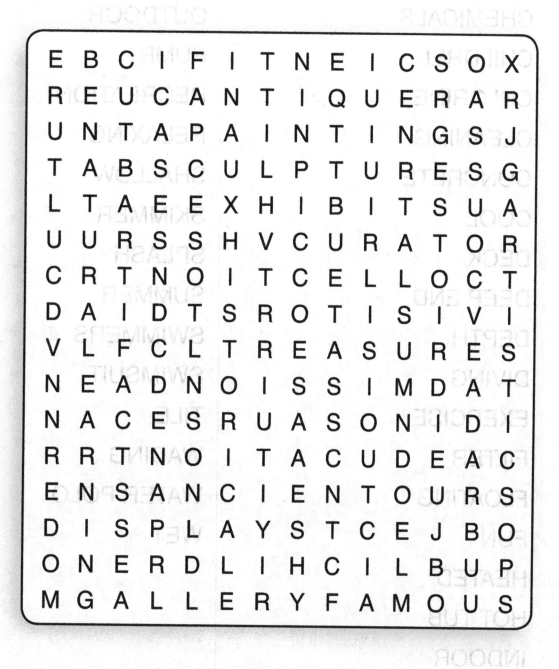

```
E B C I F I T N E I C S O X
R E U C A N T I Q U E R A R
U N T A P A I N T I N G S J
T A B S C U L P T U R E S G
L T A E E X H I B I T S U A
U U R S S H V C U R A T O R
C R T N O I T C E L L O C T
D A I D T S R O T I S I V I
V L F C L T R E A S U R E S
N E A D N O I S S I M D A T
N A C E S R U A S O N I D I
R R T N O I T A C U D E A C
E N S A N C I E N T O U R S
D I S P L A Y S T C E J B O
O N E R D L I H C I L B U P
M G A L L E R Y F A M O U S
```

Solution on Page 316

BACKSTROKE

CHEMICALS

CHILDREN

CHLORINE

CLEANING

CONCRETE

COOL

DECK

DEEP END

DEPTH

DIVING

EXERCISE

FILTER

FLOATING

FUN

HEATED

HOT TUB

INDOOR

KIDS

LADDERS

LANES

LAPS

LOUNGE

OUTDOOR

PUMP

RECREATION

RELAXING

SHALLOW

SKIMMER

SPLASH

SUMMER

SWIMMERS

SWIMSUIT

TILE

WADING

WATER POLO

WET

Motel Pool

```
G F L J G N I T A O L F L E
N G A K N R C S R E D D A L
I N P M I E H K O X L E N I
D I S D N M E S L E I P E T
A X S E A M M W O R E T S R
W A B T E U I I P C N H E Y
D L S A L S C M R I I C L C
I E R E C R A S E S R O H L
V R E H E K L U T E O I O O
I O M P T R S I A C L S T U
N O M H E K E T W D H K T N
G D I S R N I T R A C I U G
D T W A C O D E L O P M B E
E U S L N T N L D I K M F P
C O J P O E O J K J F E U D
K I D S C W I N D O O R N P
```

Solution on Page 316

ASPHALT

BRICKS

CARS

CEMENT

CINDERS

COMPOSITE

CONCRETE

CRACKS

GRANULAR

GRAVEL

HARD

HIGHWAY

HOT

ICY

LINES

MACADAM

MUD

PAVEMENT

PAVING

POTHOLE

RIDE

ROAD

ROCK

ROUGH

RUBBER

SALT

SAND

SLICK

SMOOTH

STONE

STREET

SURFACE

TARMAC

TRAFFIC

VEHICLES

WHITE

WOOD

Solution on page

Road Surface

```
Z O T S I L L S I D O O W L
M F H G U O R O A D M S H N
D A T A R M A C P N U V I U
T I D T L A S A N S D K T S
Z N Z A P V V M R X C L E B
C S E L C I H E V I A C Y G
R T L M N A D V L H C O A O
A R O G E N M S P C D N W M
C E H B I V U S B A R C H S
K E T C W R A L U N A R G K
S T O C F Z S P O X H E I G
E K P A E C I F F A R T H O
N D C C O M P O S I T E T K
I E I I A R E B B U R O C K
L C E R R R E N O T S V H N
R R Y B W B S H T O O M S Z
```

Solution on Page 317

ALPS

ARTISTS

BELGIUM

BONAPARTE

CHAMPAGNE

COUNTRY

CUISINE

CULTURE

ECONOMY

FOOD

FRANCISCA

GERMANY

GOVERNMENT

HISTORY

LANGUAGE

LITERATURE

LOIRE

LOUVRE

LOVE

LUXEMBOURG

LYON

MARIANNE

MUSEUM

NAPOLEON

PARLIAMENT

REVOLUTION

SEINE

SENATE

SPAIN

TOURISTS

TRAVEL

VERSAILLES

WINE

French Vacation

```
T  P  N  I  A  P  S  E  I  N  E  P  L  P
R  L  F  R  A  N  C  I  S  C  A  I  O  M
A  O  X  D  H  I  S  T  O  R  Y  N  U  U
V  I  R  G  N  A  P  O  L  E  O  N  V  E
E  R  A  O  R  X  M  I  U  I  J  W  R  S
L  E  R  V  A  U  A  A  T  T  E  I  E  U
Y  N  T  E  E  M  O  U  R  R  O  N  G  M
O  G  I  R  E  R  L  B  U  I  I  E  A  U
N  A  S  N  A  O  S  T  M  S  A  Y  U  I
G  P  T  M  V  P  A  A  I  E  R  N  G  G
E  M  S  E  X  R  A  U  I  T  X  Z  N  L
R  A  R  N  E  G  C  N  N  L  D  U  A  E
M  H  S  T  S  I  R  U  O  T  L  N  L  B
A  C  I  G  F  O  O  D  C  B  G  E  P  K
N  L  O  V  E  C  U  L  T  U  R  E  S  M
Y  M  O  N  O  C  E  T  A  N  E  S  L  T
```

Solution on Page 317

ADVENTURE

BACKPACK

CAJON PASS

CALIFORNIA

CANADA

CASCADE

DESERT

EQUESTRIAN

EXPLORE

FORESTS

HIKERS

HIKING

HISTORY

HORSES

LAKES

MAP

MEXICO

MOUNTAINS

OREGON

OUTDOORS

PARKS

PCT

RANGE

RECREATION

ROUTE

SCENIC

SEABOARD

SNOW

TERMINUS

TERRAIN

TRAILS

WASHINGTON

WEST

WILDERNESS

WILDLIFE

YOSEMITE

Solution on Page

Pacific Crest Trail

```
Y O S E M I T E R M I N U S
R N O G E R O F O R E S T S
O C A N A D A O C I X E M E
T P A I W A S H I N G T O N
S E L S E T U O R A A J U R
I S R E C R E A T I O N N E
H U C O L A N T N R T I T D
I B A M L G D R S T L A A L
K A J D E P O E R S W R I I
E C O N V F X S O E I R N W
R K N C I E P E O U L E S H
S P P L G A N D D Q D T C I
B A A A R P C T T E L S E K
Q C S K M Z A O U K I E N I
Q K S E S R O H O R F W I N
W O N S D R A O B A E S C G
```

Solution on Page 317

ACCIDENTS

ALASKA

ARCTIC CAT

ATV

AVALANCHE

BOMBARDIER

COLD

DANGEROUS

DEEP SNOW

DRAG RACING

DRIVER

ENGINE

EXTREME

FAST

FOREST

FOUR STROKE

FUN

GASOLINE

ICE

JUMP

LAND

LOUD

MOTOR

MOUNTAIN

NOISE

PASSENGER

PATHS

POLARIS

RIDER

SKIS

SLED

SNOWCAT

SPEED

TRACKS

TRAILS

TRANSPORT

TRAVEL

VEHICLE

WINTER

YAMAHA

Snowmobile

```
P G Y A M A H A S K I S D S
A T A K E X T E L C I H E V
T R B S A V A L A N C H E A
H I O A O V C O L D C K P F
S D M L T L C F U N O M S T
H E B A D R I V E R U D N A
T R A V E L T N T J A A O C
F O R E S T C S E C I N W W
D T D R A G R A C I N G S O
N O I S E U A I C E I E L N
A M E K O D D P O L A R I S
L E R F P E U F A S T O A K
Y T R A N S P O R T N U R C
W I N T E R D E L S U S T A
P A S S E N G E R A O M Y R
E N I G N E X T R E M E D T
```

Solution on Page 317

ART
ATLANTIC
BASQUE
BEACH
CATHOLIC
CIVIL WAR
COAST
COUNTRY
CUISINE
CULTURE
DANCE
DEMOCRACY
EUROPE
EXPLORERS
FLAMENCO
FOOTBALL
FRANCO
GAZPACHO
HISTORY
IBIZA
KINGDOM
LATIN

MONARCHY
MUSIC
PAELLA
PENINSULA
PORTUGAL
PYRENEES
RICE
ROMANCE
SEVILLE
SPANIARDS
TAPAS
TRADITION
VALENCIA
WARM
WINE

```
K I N G D O M C U L T U R E
S Y R T N U O C U I A D L U
R D A N C E C H O I P R A Q
E A T L A N T I C C S X T S
R H W E J I S N L A N I I A
O N C L Q W E D P O P A N B
L F O L I L B E A C H Z R E
P O B I A V N M E M S T A F
X O L V T I I O L U E F A G
E T A E N I M C L S E L E C
C B G S L S D R A I N A P S
I A U U R O M A N C E M O I
R L T T S A O C R X R E R B
A L R W A R M Y L T Y N U I
Y R O T S I H U K C P C E Z
S A P A T Y H C R A N O M A
```

Solution on Page 318

AIR SPORTS

AIRCRAFT

AIRPLANE

AVIATION

CONTROLS

DRAG

ENGINE

FIBERGLASS

FLIGHT

FLYING

GLIDING

HANG

HOBBY

LAND

LAUNCH

LIFT

MILITARY

MODELS

PAPER

PARACHUTE

PARAGLIDER

PILOT

RECREATION

RISING AIR

SAILPLANE

SOAR

TAIL

TOW

TRAINING

ULTRALIGHT

UNPOWERED

WEIGHT

WINGS

Glider Aircraft

```
R T F A R C R I A X A J Y J
B M I L I T A R Y Q Y F B S
S W B E T R G N I Y L F B H
Z T E V N O I T A I V A O Q
P X R I T A W A G G T L H E
L R G O G G L H G G H I A T
I P L N P H T P D N G A N U
M I A S I S T E L O I T G H
P S S R L D R T F I L S A C
V L S G A E I I H T A X I A
K O A S W G D L A A R S R R
L R A O S R L O G E T G P A
D T P A P E R I M R L N L P
G N I N I A R T D C U I A N
U O W F E N G I N E Q W N J
H C N U A L A N D R R V E T
```

Solution on Page 318

BOROUGH

CARS

CITIES

COMMUNITY

COMMUTING

DISTRICT

FAMILIES

FENCES

GRASS

HIGHWAYS

HOMES

HOUSEWIFE

HOUSING

LAND

LAWNS

MALLS

OPEN

OUTLYING

OUTSIDE

OUTSKIRTS

PARK

PEOPLE

PERFECT

POPULATION

QUIET

RICH

RURAL

SCHOOLS

SPRAWL

STREETS

STRIP MALL

SUBURBIA

TOWN

TRAFFIC

TREES

YARDS

ZONING

```
X H O L S C H O O L S P S K
B C U W F S D R A Y O A S G
P I T A A S R R A U I E P F
E R S R M A U W T B M O Q E
R F K P I R H S R O P U L N
F S I S L G I U H U I H E C
E T R W I D B O L E Y P O E
C E T H E U U A T T O M P S
T E S C S S T R I P M A L L
R R D C I I U N X U R A B W
A T B N O R U O T K W N O E
F S G N A M T I H N M W R L
F R W B M L N S S P A O O P
I A D O B G G N I Y L T U O
C C C I T I E S V D L C G E
Z O N I N G T R E E S I H P
```

Solution on Page 318

ACTIVITIES

AMENITIES

ATTRACTION

BARS

BEACHES

CARIBBEAN

CASINO

CLUB MED

DINING

EXPENSIVE

FOOD

FOREIGN

FRONT DESK

GOLF

GUESTS

HEALTH

HOLIDAYS

HOTELS

INCLUSIVE

ISLAND

MOUNTAIN

PARADISE

POOL

RECREATION

RELAXATION

RESTAURANT

SERVICE

SHOPPING

SKI RESORT

SKIING

SPA

SUN

SWIMMING

VACATION

```
C A S I N O I T A C A V I G
F L O G O A G N I I K S C U
G N I N I D M P O O L L A E
S C B T T H F E N A U C V S
Y O E R A E K U N B T I L T
A N A O X A S D M I S E N S
D C C S A L E E V U T O G E
I A H E L T D I L O I I V
L R E R E H T C H T S S E I
O I S I R I N R A P G H R S
H B I K E I O E A Z F O O N
I B D S S E R V I C E P F E
S E A X S C F O O D T P P P
V A R R E M O U N T A I N X
T N A R U A T S E R L N O E
I B P N S W I M M I N G L N
```

Solution on Page 318

ALAMO

AMUSEMENT

BEACHES

BOARDWALK

BUILDING

CALIFORNIA

CANYON

CAPE COD

CASINOS

CHICAGO

DISNEYLAND

EVERGLADES

FLORIDA

GAMBLING

HISTORY

HOLLYWOOD

LANDMARKS

LAS VEGAS

MONUMENTS

MOUNTAINS

MUSEUMS

NAVY PIER

NEW YORK

NIAGARA

ORLANDO

PARKS

PLAINS

VACATION

YOSEMITE

ZOOS

Tourist Attractions

```
R A I N R O F I L A C N H A
S M U E S U M Z O O S L O R
B U I L D I N G O O N A L A
A S N I A T N U O M I S L G
D E E J N O I T A C A V Y A
I M W C A S I N O S L E W I
R E Y O S E M I T E P G O N
O N O U K K L A W D R A O B
L T R G N I L B M A G S D E
F H K D I S N E Y L A N D A
C I S A C H I C A G O C D C
A S K L A N D M A R K S D H
N T R A M O N U M E N T S E
Y O A M R E I P Y V A N K S
O R P O T H C A P E C O D Q
N Y O R L A N D O D D D Q B S
```

Solution on Page 319

ADVENTURE	RELAXATION
AIRPLANES	ROUNDTRIP
ATTRACTION	SHIPS
AUTOMOBILE	STAY
BEACH	TOURIST
BUSINESS	TRAINS
CAMP	TRANSPORT
COMMUTING	VACATION
COUNTRIES	VISIT
DISCOVERY	WALKING
EUROPE	
GEOGRAPHY	
HIKING	
HOLIDAY	
HOTEL	
LOCATIONS	
MAPS	
MOTEL	
MOVEMENT	
PACKING	
PASSPORT	
RECREATION	

```
P V A C A T I O N K S T C P
A E U R O P E R C N R W A I
C I T M A P S O O O A S E R
K H O T E L M I P L S R S T
I P M A C M T S K P U H A D
N C O J U A N I O T I S I N
G O B T C A N R N P N S R U
E U I O R G T E S I C E P O
O N L T H T V C A O L S L R
G T E O C D N R V A G G A Y
R R I U A A T E X I N U N A
A I M R E D R A M I S D E D
P E M I B Y T T K E M I S I
H S T S A I J I T E V M T L
Y L E T O M H O H A I O A O
A B S N S S E N I S U B M H
```

Solution on Page 319

ACTIVITIES

ADVENTURER

BOLD

BOOKS

CLIMBING

DANGER

DARING

ENCOUNTER

EXCITEMENT

EXCITING

EXOTIC

EXPERIENCE

EXPLORING

EXTREME

FEAR

HIKING

JOURNEY

KNOWLEDGE

LAND

LEARNING

LIFE

NEW

PHYSICAL

RACING

RECREATION

RISKY

SKYDIVING

TRAVEL

UNUSUAL

Solution on Page

126

Adventure Travel

```
N W Q A N E X C I T I N G X
Y K S I R W Y E N R U O J S
D L O B E X P E R I E N C E
N A O K R O M J F Q W G X G
A L R V U E O D A N G E R N
L S E I T I V I T C A N N I
I I B I N O I T A E R C E R
F R C E E G O L G P A O X O
E X W A V L E D C F C U O L
E N U A D V E L E N I N T P
M Z N W A L I A A W N T I X
E H V R W M R G R U G E C E
R X T O B O O K S N S R R X
T G N I V I D Y K S I U G L
X K N P H Y S I C A L N N B
E G N I K I H Q Y L Q R G U
```

Solution on Page 319

BICYCLES

BIKE

CANOEING

CART

CLIMBING

CRAWLING

CYCLING

ENERGY

EXERCISE

GONDOLA

HANDCAR

ICE SKATE

KAYAKING

LEISURE

MUSCLES

PEDAL

PUSHING

RICKSHAW

ROW BOAT

ROWING

RUNNING

SCOOTER

SKATEBOARD

SPRINTING

SWIMMING

TECHNOLOGY

TRANSPORT

TRICYCLE

UNICYCLE

WALKING

WHEELCHAIR

Human Powered

```
S E L C S U M K E N E R G Y
W G N I K L A W R O W I N G
I S R V H Y A L O D N O G Z
M R E Y A H A N D C A R C F
M U S K S B I C Y C L E S U
I N I K R E T O O C S K N N
N N C W H E E L C H A I R I
G I R L S P R I N T I N G C
R N E E T A K S E C I Z N Y
O G X F G N I B M I L C I C
W T E C H N O L O G Y W L L
B I K E C A N O E I N G W E
O D P T R O P S N A R T A T
A L A D E P K L E I S U R E
T R I C Y C L E T S W A C A
P U S H I N G N I L C Y C D
```

Solution on Page 319

ALEXANDRIA

AMERICA

ARLINGTON

ATTRACTION

COLONIAL

DISTILLERY

ESTATE

FAIRFAX

FAMILY

FARM

GARDENS

GEORGE

GIFT SHOP

GROUNDS

HISTORICAL

HOME

HOUSE

LANDMARK

MANSION

MARTHA

MONUMENT

NATIONAL

PADDOCK

PARK

PLANTATION

PRESIDENT

PROPERTY

RESIDENCE

STABLE

TOMB

VIRGINIA

WASHINGTON

WOOD

Mount Vernon

```
T H P A R K R A M D N A L P
G E O R G E C N E D I S E R
H D I S T I L L E R Y B S O
V I R G I N I A D N M Q U P
A Y S S O F W N H O M T O E
C H A T T R A C T I O N H R
I B H A O X S O B T N E L T
R L T B E R H G M A U D A Y
E A R L O F I A M T M I N F
M I A E A F N C R N E S O A
A N M M T S G E A A N E I I
J O I S I E T L F L T R T R
V L H O M A O I W P W P A F
Y O N O T G N I L R A O N A
P C H S K K C O D D A P O X
S N E D R A G R O U N D S D
```

Solution on Page 320

ARCTIC OCEAN

ATLANTIC OCEAN

BLUE

BOAT

CORAL

CRABS

CURRENTS

DEEP

DEPTH

DOLPHINS

EXPLORATION

FLOOR

GULF

HURRICANE

HYDROSPHERE

INDIAN OCEAN

ISLANDS

LARGE

MARINE

OCEANOGRAPHY

PACIFIC OCEAN

PLANKTON

PORT

SALINE

SALT WATER

SEA LIFE

SHIP

SHORE

SOUTHERN OCEAN

SURFACE

TRAVEL

TRENCHES

VAST

WHALES

Ocean Voyage

```
T E G I I S L A N D S X N E
R R T U N L E V A R T A T X
D E O R L D P E E D E S R P
E H N P E F I F C C A U E L
P P T I L N I A O V M R T O
T S A O L L C C N A F F A R
H O O C A A I H R O P A W A
U R B E I T S I E I C C T T
R D S D N F N W H S B E L I
R Y X A Q E I S T G L S A O
I H L A R G E C U W U B S N
C T A R C T I C O C E A N N
A C U R R E N T S C O R A L
N Y H P A R G O N A E C O F
E R O H S L N O T K N A L P
W H A L E S D O L P H I N S
```

Solution on Page 320

ANIMALS

ATTRACTIONS

BISON

BOATING

BUFFALO

CABIN

CALDERA

CAMPING

DEER

DESTINATION

ECOSYSTEMS

ELK

FAMOUS

FLORA

GEOTHERMAL

HIKING

HOT SPRINGS

IDAHO

LAKES

MOOSE

MOUNTAINS

NATURE

OLD FAITHFUL

PROTECTED

RIVERS

TOURISTS

TRAILS

VISITORS

WATERFALLS

WILDERNESS

WILDLIFE

WOLVES

Yellowstone National Park

```
T G Z S S E N R E D L I W M
R R C H L G L A K E S O O M
A E A W U N N Z T N R U L C
I S M M F I O I O U N E V A
L L P S H B I I R T R G E L
S L I T T A T V A P V E S D
L A N S I C A I B L S O E E
A F G I A S N C O L D T C R
M R S R F S I N A E E H O A
I E T U D M T H T F B E S H
N T L O L N S C I A U R Y I
A A Y T O R E L N M F M S K
R W Q S E T D L G O F A T I
O U I V O L M M K U A L E N
L B I R I D A H O S L E M G
F R P W R V I S I T O R S B
```

Solution on Page 320

APPETIZER

BANQUET

BREAKFAST

BRUNCH

BUFFET

CAFETERIAS

COOKING

COURSE

CUISINE

DESSERT

DINNER

DRINK

EATING

FAST FOOD

FRUIT

FULL

HOLIDAYS

HOMES

KITCHEN

LEFTOVERS

LIGHT

LUNCH

MEAT

NUTRITION

PICNIC

PREPARE

RESTAURANT

SALAD

SHARE

SIDE DISH

SNACK

SOUP

SUPPER

VEGETABLE

WINE

Stop for a Bite

```
P C P B C D E T D I N N E R
I S U A G S R E V O T F E L
C Y O N D E A F S Y H Z L F
N A S Q O M P F I U I J B W
I D F U O O E U D T P F A K
C I K E F H R B E N D P T N
K L I T T B P P D A X H E I
C O T N S E P E I R D C G R
A H C U A A R N S U E N E D
N P H T F X I I H A S U V X
S D E R A H S W A T S L G H
J G N I K O O C D S E L D F
M E A T S A F K A E R B R U
K E N I S I U C L R T U W L
K T C O U R S E A T I N G L
J H C N U R B Y S T H G I L
```

Solution on Page 320

ATHLETICS

CARDIO

DISTANCE

ENDURANCE

ENERGY

EVENTS

EXERCISE

FAST

FEET

FITNESS

FOOT

HEALTH

HURDLES

JOGGING

KNEE

LAPS

LEGS

LOCOMOTION

MARATHONS

MILE

MUSCLE

OLYMPICS

PACE

QUADRICEPS

RACING

RUN

SHOES

SOCKS

SPEED

SPORTS

SPRINTING

STREET

STRIDE

SWEAT

TIME

TRAINING

TREADMILL

WALKING

Run Away

```
S G E L T I M E D X Y B V X
O N R S T R O P S T N E V E
C I P A C E N D U R A N C E
K G D B Q E E H V O O N E S
S G F R U S U R L I A N A I
W O I U A R N Y T T K T G C
E J T N D C M O S S H N L R
A F N L R P M I H L I A L E
T A E E I O D D E T P I I X
E S S C C S E T N S A U M E
E T S O E E I I Y E Q R D B
F D L O P C R G N I K L A W
C J H S S P R M U S C L E M
O S U Q S E G N I N I A R T
R A C I N G S S H E A L T H
M I L E D I R T S F O O T I
```

Solution on Page 321

AIRPLANE	KITCHENS
ALCOHOL	KOSHER
BEEF	LUNCH
BEVERAGE	MEAT
BLAND	NAPKIN
BOX	PEPPER
BREAKFAST	PLASTIC
CART	PRETZELS
CATERING	QUALITY
CHICKEN	ROLL
CHOICE	SALT
COFFEE	SERVICE
CUTLERY	SMALL
DESSERT	SNACK
DRINK	SPORK
ECONOMY	STEAK
FISH	TRAVEL
FOOD	WATER
FREE	
FROZEN	
HOT	
IN-FLIGHT	

Airline Meals

```
Q V E K G G T O H C O I R Q
R F R O Z E N C H O I C E S
R F I S H U N I E X N J P J
X O B H E U C G R I Y O P E
K O D E L K A N K E R T E C
A D E R E R R P O K T S P I
E S S N E N A L P R I A N V
T B S V M N V C N A D F C R
S P E C O N O M Y N L K A E
A B R E R F A T A I I A R S
L M T E F I I L G T K E T N
T E T E T L B H C N W R R A
O A E W A Z T H I O F B A C
W T C U T L E R Y B H R V K
K F Q Q J N D L L O R O E W
L L A M S P L A S T I C L E
```

Solution on Page 321

ASHEVILLE

BARBECUE

BASKETBALL

BEACHES

BOBCATS

CARDINAL

CAROLINA

CHAPEL HILL

COLONY

CONFEDERATE

COTTON

DOGWOOD

EAST COAST

FLIGHT

FORT BRAGG

FURNITURE

GOLF

GREENSBORO

HISTORIC

HURRICANES

KITTY HAWK

MT. MITCHELL

OUTER BANKS

PANTHERS

PINE

RALEIGH

SAND

SOUTHERN

WILMINGTON

North Carolina

```
S K J N O T G N I M L I W Q
E I O E F R S O U T H E R N
N T T U E Q O A F L I G H T
A T W S T A C B O B M S G P
C Y G T A E P I S C B D I E
I H G E R F R A R N T N E L
R A A H E H S B N O E S L B
R W R P D E E E A T T E A H
U K B C E F R U H N H S R E
H D T A F L J U C C K E I G
C O R R N O H C T E A S R H
O O O D O G K I T I B E J S
T W F I C Y M B L G N R B X
T G F N F T A N I L O R A C
O O D A M L C O L O N Y U B
N D E L L I V E H S A N D F
```

Solution on Page 321

BALLAST

BOILER

BOOSTER

BOXCAR

BUFFER

CABOOSE

CARS

COAL

COUPLER

DIESEL

EXPRESS

FIREBOX

FIREMAN

FLATCAR

FREIGHT

GAUGE

GONDOLA

HANDCAR

LANTERN

LINE

LOOP

PISTON

RAILCAR

RAILROAD

RAILWAY

ROUTE

SIGNAL

SLEEPER

SPIKES

STATIONS

STEEL

SUBWAY

SWITCH

TICKETS

TIES

TOKEN

TRACKS

TRAINS

WHEELS

WHISTLE

Railroad Words

```
D I E S E L A N G I S E I T
A A B T O K E N K V C F F M
O P O O L R A C X O B I T J
R E O D R E F F U B R R S W
L G S S E R P X E A E E H
I U T S A L L A B I I M K E
A A E N A E L O N T L A I E
R G R O R E X S C Y W N P L
E O C I E C F A N T A O S S
P N C T R L B R R B Y T T B
E D S A A O A A E O G S E G
E O E T O C C I T I B I K L
L L C S D K A L N L G P C I
S A E N S T R C A E B H I N
R Y A W B U S A L R O U T E
W H I S T L E R S W I T C H
```

Solution on Page 321

AIRCRAFT

AIRPLANE

BICYCLES

BOATS

BRIDGES

BUSES

CARS

DEPOT

DRIVER

FARE

FERRY

FREIGHT

FUEL

GAS

GOODS

HIGHWAYS

HORSE

JET

METRO

MONORAIL

MOVEMENT

PEOPLE

PUBLIC

RAILROAD

ROADS

ROCKET

SAILBOAT

SHIPS

SPEED

TERMINALS

TRACKS

TRAFFIC

TRAINS

TRAVEL

TRUCKS

VAN

VEHICLES

WALKING

WATER

WHEELS

Solution on

```
K T Z X M P F U E L A S E G
W H E E L S E E V T D B N T
S S T J N M D O R E V I R D
F R E I G H T A P R K C H T
O E A G Q W C O O L Y Y U E
G R R C D K T S A R E C S K
T T B A S I Y W P U B L I C
M A R T F A R C R I A E S O
E O L A W Q L B T N I S H R
S B V H I B I R I S R E I E
R L G E U L A M L A P L P T
O I N S M F R B E G L C S A
H A E Y F E O O V O A I V W
V S C I T C N A A O N H M Q
S K C U R T O T R D E E P S
L Z Q J R Q M S T S E V G J
```

Solution on Page 322

AIRPORT

AMUSEMENT PARK

ANIMAL KINGDOM

ATTRACTIONS

BEACH

CITY

DESTINATION

DISNEY WORLD

DOWNTOWN

ENTERTAINMENT

FAMILY

FUN

HEAT

HOTELS

HUMID

HURRICANE

MAGIC KINGDOM

METROPOLITAN

OCEAN

ORANGE COUNTY

ORLANDO MAGIC

RESORT

ROLLER COASTER

SENTINEL

SUN BELT

THEME PARKS

TRAVEL

WALT DISNEY

```
H U R R I C A N E T A E H D
M N W O T N W O D H T D V E
O O S U N B E L T E T L K S
R Y D B E A C H S M R R N T
L E C G M F U N L E A O A I
A N T D N M B M E P C W T N
N S R S I I C L T A T Y I A
D I O D A I K N O R I E L T
O D P Q T O E C H K O N O I
M T R Y R M C G I S N S P O
A L I L E V A R T G S I O N
G A A S T R O S E R A D R A
I W U Q N F A M I L Y M T E
C M Q S E N T I N E L Q E C
A N I M A L K I N G D O M O
G P Y T N U O C E G N A R O
```

Solution on Page 322

AMERICAS

ATLANTIC

CAPTAIN

COLONIZER

DISCOVERY

ENGLAND

EUROPE

EXPEDITION

EXPLORER

FERDINAND

FLAT

GENOA

HISPANIOLA

HISTORY

HOLIDAY

INDIANS

ISABELLA

ITALIAN

NAVIGATOR

NEW WORLD

NINA

OCEAN

OCTOBER

PORTUGAL

QUEEN

SAILING

SEA

SHIPS

SPAIN

SPICES

TRADING

TRAVEL

VOYAGES

Christopher Columbus

```
C Y D E X P E D I T I O N T
E F I N I A P S H D T R A F
Z L S D A G R K I L A S V A
E A C N I N A O S R L N I E
U T O A V I I A T O I A G S
R H V L C L C D O W A I A P
O O E G G I E S R W N D T I
P L R N R A T V Y E A N O H
E I Y E I S O N A N F I R S
F D M K Z S P N A R C A E E
N A E C O I A I E L T T R G
J Y Q U E E N B C G T P O A
T R E B O T C O E E X A L Y
Y P O R T U G A L L S C P O
D U H I S P A N I O L A X V
L K T R A D I N G C C A E Y
```

Solution on Page 322

BANJO

BEBOP

BIG BAND

BOB DYLAN

BROADWAY

CHRISTIAN

CLASSICAL

CONCERTS

DANCE

DRUMS

FOLK

FUSION

GENRE

GOSPEL

GRUNGE

GUITAR

HARD ROCK

HAWAIIAN

HIP HOP

INDIE

JAZZ

MEMPHIS

MOTOWN

MTV

NASHVILLE

ORCHESTRA

PATRIOTIC

POP

PUNK ROCK

RADIO

RAGTIME

RECORD

REGGAE

RHYTHM

SINGERS

SOUL

SWING

SYMPHONY

TECHNO

Car Radio Music

```
R E S I H P M E M E D K L V
M A M O T O W N F C N C B G
H G U T F H R U O N A O Z B
T G R O V P S T L A B R Z E
Y E D G N I W S K D G K A B
H R Y N O H P M Y S I N J O
R E P N N C L Q C B U N P
A C M B A A A E S L E P A A
T O W I R N S I T A I O I T
I R H P T O N H T S D I I R
U D R O S G A N V S N D A I
G O S P E L A D J I I A W O
E J S R H C B R W C L R A T
N N S K C O R D R A H L H I
R A L G R U N G E L Y U E C
E B I C O N C E R T S O U L
```

Solution on Page 322

APPETIZER

BALANCE

BANQUET

BREAKFAST

BRUNCH

BUFFET

CALORIE

CHEESE

CHEWING

COOK

CUISINE

DESSERT

DIET

DIGESTION

DINING

DINNER

DRINK

ENERGY

FRUIT

GROWTH

HEALTHY

HERBIVORE

HUNGER

INGESTION

INTAKE

LUNCH

NUTRITION

OBESITY

OMNIVORES

PASTA

PLATE

SNACKING

SWALLOWING

VEGETABLES

Eating on the Road

```
P H E A L T H Y U M E F P Y
L G N O I T I R T U N N G T
A R I T R E S S E D R R R I
T O S E L B A T E G E V E U
E W I I S F R L N N Z L G R
U T U D K E D I E D I N N F
Q H C A N S W J I R T O U T
N Z E N M O E N B I E I H A
A R I R L G I R N N P T C Y
B D B L B N G T O K P S N T
P Q A E G I A N S V A E U I
A W L S W K V V I E I G L S
S W A E E C O O K W G N Z E
T L N E C A L O R I E I M B
A G C H C N U R B E Y H D O
U F E C F S B U F F E T C Z
```

Solution on Page 323

AIR FORCE

APOLLO

ASTRONAUTS

BASE

CHALLENGER

COLUMBIA

COUNTDOWN

DISCOVERY

EXPLORE

FLIGHTS

FLORIDA

GEMINI

GOVERNMENT

HISTORY

KENNEDY

LAUNCH PAD

LIFTOFF

MARS

MERCURY

MISSIONS

MOON

NASA

ORBITER

ORLANDO

ROCKETS

SATELLITE

SATURN

SCIENCE

SHUTTLES

SKY

SPACE

TECHNOLOGY

TOURS

TRAINING

Kennedy Space Center

```
E C A P S C I E N C E S A B
F L I G H T S H U T T L E S
S R A M I S S I O N S I R T
F L O R I D A K E A Y F O E
A P O L L O A M Y S G T L K
S A T U R N N P L A O O P C
T Y R U C R E M H C L F X O
R E G N E L L A H C O F E R
O G C V O N W O D T N U O C
N O O M Y R O T S I H U O O
A G L V A I R F O R C E A R
U E U T D I S C O V E R Y L
T M M T E T I L L E T A S A
S I B K E N N E D Y A W E N
G N I N I A R T O U R S I D
F I A O R B I T E R O W R O
```

Solution on Page 323

AUGUSTA

BIRDIE

BOGEY

CADDIES

CART

CHIP

CLUBS

COURSES

DRIVER

EAGLE

EIGHTEEN

FAIRWAY

FLAGS

GAME

GRASS

GREENS

HANDICAP

HAZARD

HOLES

IRONS

LEISURE

MASTERS

MATCH

PAR

PGA

PIN

PLAYERS

PUTTER

ROUGH

SAND TRAP

SCOTLAND

SHOES

SPORT

STROKE

SWING

TEES

WALK

WATER

WEDGE

WOODS

```
E G D E W O O D S Q K C T R
L R M G R R O U G H S N R W
M A G R S E I D D A C C A A
G S T R O K E S T Y O T C L
A S H O E S C S D U E S A K
Y E M A C E U L R R U G H M
K W A S N G N S U U I D O N
F K S G U D E S M B D V L B
P F T A L S I F C N S Z E D
X V E L N E G C A H B N S R
H P R F L D H L A I I I R A
Y P S P U T T E R P R P E Z
B Y N Z G O E R U U D W Y A
B O O Z C A E E A U I G A H
E Z R S W I N G S P E K L Y
F W I O O E R O G T R O P S
```

Solution on Page 323

BICYCLE

BIKE

BOX

BUSINESS

CARRIER

CITY

COMPANY

DELIVERY

DHL

DISTANCE

DOCUMENTS

EXPENSIVE

EXPRESS

FAST

FEDEX

IMPORTANT

MAIL

MESSAGES

MESSENGER

OFFICE

OVERNIGHT

PACKAGES

PARCEL

PERSON

PIGEON

ROUTE

RUNNER

SCALES

SECURITY

SEND

SERVICES

SIGNATURE

SPEED

TRACKING

TRANSPORT

TRAVEL

TYPEFACE

UPS

VAN

```
F E D E X B U S I N E S S R
A B K I M P O R T A N T I E
S E L A C S P U D X N H G N
T E X P E N S I V E C G N N
R E G N E S S E M N O I A U
A D H L S T S U O F W N T R
C N P Y A E C E F T X R U Y
K E A N J O G I R T O E R Q
I S C A D I C A L P B V E N
N E K P P E V G S E X O I O
G R A M W E L N D S C E R S
V V G O L R A I U P E R R R
G I E C O R O N V E L M A E
Q C S Y T I R U C E S I C P
N E L C Y C I B T D R N A V
B S B I K E C A F E P Y T M
```

Solution on Page 323

ACTION

BACCARAT

BETTING

BLACKJACK

BROKE

CHANCE

CONCERTS

CRAPS

FUN

GAMBLING

GAMING

HAND

HOTELS

INDIAN

LAS VEGAS

MACHINES

MIRAGE

MONACO

NEVADA

ODDS

PEOPLE

PIT

PLAYER

POKER

RENO

RESORT

RESTAURANT

REVENUE

ROULETTE

SECURITY

SHOPPING

SLOT

SPORTS

TABLES

TOURIST

WIN

Solution on Page

Puzzles

Casino

```
O C A N O M N E V A D A O T
D P Q S S E G A R I M E I T
D E R H E R E N O T U F O R
S O E O C W Z J I N N U K O
W P Y P U B S P E M R C S S
M L A P R L R V F I A O P E
I E L I I Z E O S J B G O R
N C P N T R S T K N E Q R E
D N B G Y S T C T E T S T K
I A M A D N A H Y E T E S O
A H H M C L U G Z R I N E P
N C O B B C R A E W N I L N
I R T L Y F A C G V G H B H
W A E I U M N R X C S C A A
G P L N O O T T A N C A T D
H S S G C N S L O T J M L E
```

Solution on Page 324

AIR FILTER

BEARINGS

BODY WORK

BUGGY

CABRIOLET

COMPACTS

CORVAIR

CV JOINT

DEFROSTER

FUEL PUMP

GAS GAUGE

GASKETS

HEADLIGHTS

HOT ROD

HUB CAPS

ODOMETER

OIL CHANGE

PONY CAR

RAGTOP

REST STOPS

ROAD SIGNS

STRUTS

STUDEBAKER

TACHOMETER

THROTTLE

TRANS AM

TRANSAXLE

TUNE UP

V ENGINE

VW BUS

WOODIE

```
I V W B U S T C A P M O C E
G A S K E T S P O N Y C A R
R I A V R O C Y Y G G U B V
E I D O O W B O D Y W O R K
A T A C H O M E T E R I I S
R S T U D E B A K E R L O T
E E J O D O M E T E R C L R
T L S T H G I L D A E H E U
S X G T E N I G N E V A T T
O A A T S F B E A R I N G S
R S S N R T U N E U P G H P
F N G I P O T G A R E O A
E A A O P M U P L E U F T C
D R U J S N G I S D A O R B
Q T G V E L T T O R H T O U
M R E C T R A N S A M D D H
```

Solution on Page 324

ANIMALS

BEARS

BIKING

CANYONS

EL CAPITAN

FIRE

FOREST

FUN

GEOLOGY

HABITAT

HALF DOME

HISTORY

JOHN MUIR

LAKES

MADERA

MOUNTAINS

NATURE

PLANTS

PROTECTED

RANGERS

RECREATION

SEQUOIAS

STREAMS

SUBALPINE

TOURISTS

TRAILS

TUOLUMNE

USA

VALLEY

VEGETATION

VISITORS

VOLCANO

WATERFALLS

WILDERNESS

WILDLIFE

Scenic Yosemite

```
L C M G E O L O G Y S K U U
A F O R E S T A T I B A H N
K B I S E Q U O I A S U A M
E F T U O L U M N E J Q L O
S R U D E T C E T O R P F U
W R E N I P L A B U S N D N
V I S I T O R S P E O U O T
Y U L T R A I L S I A I M A
R M A D R A V L T R T R E I
O N M D E O A A R A O A S N
T H I Y L R T F E N U G N S
S O N C E E N R A G R N O T
I J A D G L C E M E I I Y N
H N A E R E L T S R S K N A
O M V E R U T A N S T I A L
E F I L D L I W V P S B C P
```

Solution on Page 324

ATLANTIC	RIVER
BANK	ROCKY
BEACHES	SAND
BOAT	SEAGULLS
BORDER	SEAWEED
CALIFORNIA	SHORE
CLIFFS	SUNBATHING
CORAL	SURFING
COVE	SWIMMING
DOCK	TIDES
EAST COAST	TOURISTS
EROSION	VIEW
FISHING	WATER
GULF	WAVES
HARBOR	WEST
INLET	ZONE
LAND	
LEVEE	
MAP	
OCEANS	
PACIFIC	
PORT	

Coastline

```
W D P O R T Q G C S A N D S
E O D O F B Q O W W A V E S
S C C T O U R I S T S D F S
T K U R A A M F D R I X E H
Y E D S L M A P N T I H Q S
K E L U I N N U A S C V N H
R A I N R O F I L A C A E O
G Y G B I I V Y E O E X B R
N F C A R S A B D C H R O E
I L I T O O S T O T O B A E
F E F H G R F I L S R V T C
R V I I K E F S E A W E E D
U E C N G K I W H E N O Z C
S E A G U L L S E W A T E R
L B P K L H C G N I H S I F
K H Z G F E M J R D V X D C
```

Solution on Page 324

ARCHITECTURE

BASKETBALL

BEN FRANKLIN

BETSY ROSS

BROTHERLY LOVE

CITY

CONSTITUTION

DELAWARE RIVER

EAGLES

FAIRMOUNT PARK

FRESH PRINCE

GREEN

HISTORY

INDEPENDENCE

INQUIRER

LIBERTY BELL

MARKET STREET

MINT

NORTH

PARKS

POPULATION

ROCKY

SOCIETY HILL

UNITED STATES

UNIVERSITY

URBAN

Philadelphia

```
E B N I L K N A R F N E B F
R R B B C R I G P T S V S D
U F A E O O V H O N K O E I
T R S T N C X I P I R L T N
C E K S S K S S U M A Y A D
E S E Y T Y O T L W P L T E
T H T R I T C O A M T R S P
I P B O T I I R T I N E D E
H R A S U S E Y I N U H E N
C I L S T R T S O Q O T T D
R N L G I E Y E N U M O I E
A C A V O V H L K I R R N N
O E E B N I I G C R I B U C
G R E E N N L A I E A C A E
N O R T H U L E T R F M Z N
W E L I B E R T Y B E L L M
```

Solution on Page 325

ACROPOLIS

AEGEAN SEA

ALEXANDER

ANCIENT

ARISTOTLE

ATHENS

CLASSICAL

CRETE

CUISINE

CYPRUS

DEMOCRACY

DRAMA

EUROPEAN

GODS

HELLENIC

HOMER

LANGUAGE

LITERATURE

MACEDONIA

MOUNTAINS

MYTHOLOGY

OLIVE OIL

ORTHODOX

PARTHENON

PENINSULA

PHILOSOPHY

REPUBLIC

SPARTA

TRAVEL

TURKEY

WINE

ZEUS

Greece

```
S M O E L T O T S I R A M W
U Y D N A L E X A N D E R S
R T R E P U B L I C R S E N
P H A N M Y E K R U T N G I
Y O M I G O D S T W S A A A
C L A S S I C A L I T E U T
O O H I O R R R L R N G G N
R G H U Z E H O A I T E N U
T Y Y C T M P P W C X A A O
H P H I L O S O P H Y S L M
O O L Q R H E L L E N I C S
D M A C E D O N I A V H G N
O H A T P A R T H E N O N E
X Z E U S E U R O P E A N H
I R A L U S N I N E P R V T
C T R A V E L T N E I C N A
```

Solution on Page 325

AXLE

BIG RIG

BOX TRUCK

BROKER

CARRIER

CONSIGNOR

CONTAINER

CONVOY

DEMURRAGE

DIESEL

DOCK

DRIVER

ENGINE

FLATBED

FREIGHT

FUEL

GAS

INDUSTRY

KINGPIN

LOG BOOK

MANIFEST

OVERSIZE

PALLET

RADIO

RECEIVER

ROAD

ROUTE

SEMI

SHIPMENT

SHIPPER

SLEEPER

TANDEM

TERMINAL

TRACTOR

TRAILER

TRANSPORT

TRUCK STOP

TRUCKLOAD

Trucking Words

```
R E L I A R T A T T L B T E
P T H G I E R F R R E R A S
T S E F I N A M U A U O N H
K H N L Y S N K C C F K D I
I I G A R A S B K T O E E P
N P I T T G P L S O L R M P
G M N B S B O X T R U C K E
P E E E U A R R O A D O K R
I N O D D X T U P E R N O E
N T V B N L T D M E Y S O V
D P E I I E O U P O E I B I
R A R G M C R E V M A G G E
I L S R K R E N I A T N O C
V L I I A L O I D A R O L E
E E Z G S C A R R I E R U R
R T E R M I N A L E S E I D
```

Solution on Page 325

AIRPORTS
ART
BANKS
BEIJING
BUSINESS
CENTER
CHICAGO
CULTURAL
DIVERSE
ECONOMY
FINANCE
GEOGRAPHY
HISTORY
HONG KONG
IMPORTANT
INFLUENCE
LARGE
LONDON
MEGACITY
METROPOLIS
MOSCOW
NEW YORK

OPERA
PARIS
POLITICAL
POPULATION
ROME
SEOUL
SHANGHAI
SINGAPORE
SYDNEY
TORONTO
TRAFFIC
URBAN
WORLD CITY

Global Cities

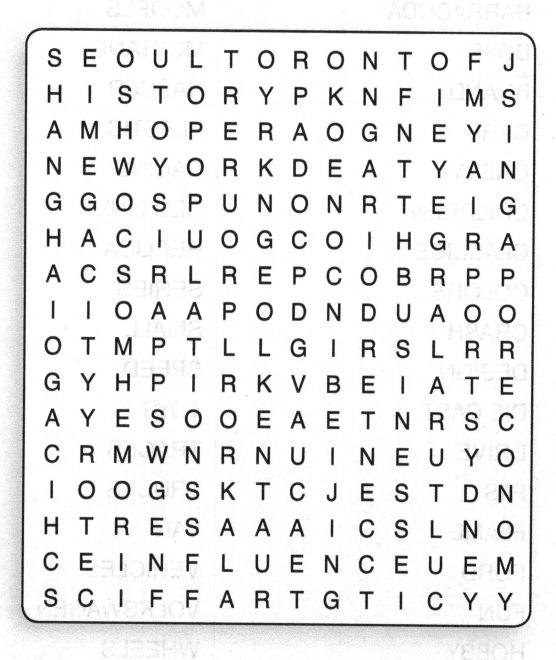

```
S E O U L T O R O N T O F J
H I S T O R Y P K N F I M S
A M H O P E R A O G N E Y I
N E W Y O R K D E A T Y A N
G G O S P U N O N R T E I G
H A C I U O G C O I H G R A
A C S R L E P C O B R P P
I I O A A P O D N D U A O O
O T M P T L L G I R S L R R
G Y H P I R K V B E I A T E
A Y E S O O E A E T N R S C
C R M W N R N U I N E U Y O
I O O G S K T C J E S T D N
H T R E S A A A I C S L N O
C E I N F L U E N C E U E M
S C I F F A R T G T I C Y Y
```

Solution on Page 325

AMERICAN

BARRACUDA

BOYS

BRAND

CARS

CHEVY

CHILDREN

CLASSICS

COLORS

CRASH

DESIGN

DIE CAST

DRIVE

FAST

FLAME

FORD

FUN

HOBBY

HOT RODS

KIDS

MATCHBOX

MATTEL

METAL

MODELS

MUSTANG

NASCAR

PLASTIC

RACING

RED LINE

REPLICA

SERIES

SMALL

SPEED

TOYS

TRACKS

TRUCKS

VAN

VEHICLES

VOLKSWAGEN

WHEELS

Hot Wheels

```
G V O W M S E I R E S R V S
D E W H U M S K C A R T M P
E H D E S I G N A S C A R Y
E I Y E T D N A R B L I B T
P C V L A M O D E L S B N F
S L E S N K S R O L O C O G
E E H M G E B P T H X R T E
S S C I S S A L C O D N S N
Y D F U N E R D L I H C A I
A C I L P E R S Y O T C C L
V O L K S W A G E N I N E D
P L A S T I C C S R A C I E
F L A M E R U Y E V I R D R
P M E T A L D M A T T E L R
B O Y S O M A T C H B O X U
O O H H S K C U R T S A F A
```

Solution on Page 326

ADVENTURE	PEDALS
BALANCE	PROTECTION
BICYCLES	RACING
BIKES	RUGGED
BMX	SHOES
BRAKES	SINGLETRACK
CLIMB	SKILL
CYCLING	SPEED
DANGEROUS	SPORTS
DOWNHILL	STEEP
ENDURANCE	STRENGTH
EQUIPMENT	SUSPENSION
EXTREME	TREK
FIRE ROADS	TRIALS
FITNESS	
FREERIDE	
GEARS	
GLOVES	
HELMETS	
INJURY	
MOUNTAINS	
OFF ROAD	

Mountain Biking

```
B I K E S N I A T N U O M K
G P G Y R U J N I S A T B E
D E E S T R O P S R R R F X
A D V E N T U R E A A I R T
O A G N T X W O E E C A E R
R L E O K S F T N G I L E E
F S Q I H E I E D B N S R M
F S U S T L R C U R G A I E
O S I N G L E T R A C K D C
S E P E N I R I A K C G E N
H N M P E H O O N E O N K A
O T E S R N A N C S K I L L
E I N U T W D S E V O L G A
S F T S S O S E L C Y C I B
R U G G E D E E P S L Y H M
H E L M E T S B M I L C E X
```

Solution on Page 326

BIG MAC

BREAKFAST

BURGER KING

CALORIES

CHAINS

CHEAP

CONVENIENCE

DINNER

DRIVE THRU

FISH

FRANCHISE

FRENCH FRIES

FRIED CHICKEN

GREASE

HAMBURGERS

HOT DOGS

KFC

LUNCH

MCDONALD'S

MEALS

MENU

ORDER

PITAS

PIZZA HUT

PREPARED

RESTAURANTS

SANDWICHES

SERVICE

SUPER SIZE

TACO BELL

TRANS FAT

WHITE CASTLE

```
A F I S H T R A N S F A T A
N R E S T A U R A N T S A I
S E H C I W D N A S P L C T
E N K M E A L S G O D T O H
I C H C N U L C A M G I B L
R H W H I T E C A S T L E J
O F E S I H C N A R F O L B
L R P I D E C I V R E S L M
A I R E D R O D I N N E R C
C E E C N E I N E V N O C D
H S P A E H C V P I T A S O
A P A G N I K R E G R U B N
I B R E A K F A S T K F C A
N M E N U P I Z Z A H U T L
S M D H A M B U R G E R S D
G R E A S E Z I S R E P U S
```

Solution on Page 326

ANCIENT

ANTIQUITY

AURORA

CHICHEN ITZA

CN TOWER

COLOSSUS

EARTH

EGYPT

GREAT PYRAMID

GREAT WALL

HAGIA SOPHIA

HANGING GARDENS

HOOVER DAM

LEANING TOWER

MANMADE

MAUSOLEUM

MEDIEVAL WORLD

MOUNT EVEREST

PANAMA CANAL

PETRA

PYRAMID OF GIZA

SEVEN

SPECTACULAR

STATUE OF ZEUS

VICTORIA FALLS

Wonders of the World

```
F P G S P E C T A C U L A R
J T R Z Y E A R T H W C D G
S N E D R A G G N I G N A H
C E A L A I Y T S C M T M T
O I T R M H T D M H L O A S
L C W O I P I I A E A W D E
O N A W D O U M U N N E R R
S A L L O S Q A S I A R E E
S L L A F A I R O T C I V V
U N A V G I T Y L Z A E O E
S E R E I G N P E A M G O T
A V O I Z A A T U A A Y H N
R E R D A H K A M Q N P D U
T S U E Z F O E U T A T S O
E D A M N A M R L M P M D M
P L E A N I N G T O W E R F
```

Solution on Page 326

AMENITIES

ANCHOR

BAR

CABINS

COMFORT

CREW

CRUISING

DECK

ENGINE

EXPENSIVE

FAST

FISHING

FUEL

GALLEY

HARBOR

HUGE

HULL TYPE

LARGE

LEISURE

LUXURIOUS

MAST

MOTOR

OCEAN

PRIVATE

PROPULSION

RACING

RECREATION

RICH

SAILBOAT

SAILING

SEA

SHIP

SHORE

SPORT

STEAMBOAT

VESSEL

WATERCRAFT

WEALTHY

WEEKENDER

Yachting

```
H E R U S I E L S H O R E Z
U N E T Q F Y E L L A G W F
G I D S U O I R U X U L A W
E G N A R T O P R I V A T E
H N E F I O B L T C P G E A
C E K N O I T A E R C E R L
I V E W I O O O O U V P C T
R M E T S B C P M I F Y R H
A R W S M G U E S S F T A Y
C P A A S L N N A I D L F H
A O E M S E E I S N E L T A
E T M I K P L H L G C U S R
S G O F X B I T V I K H P B
H N R E O N S N I B A C O O
I W H A G R A C I N G S R R
P V T R L C T B A R I X T D
```

Solution on Page 327

AIR HOST
AIRCREW
AIRLINES
AIRPLANE
AIRPORT
AISLE
AVIATION
BOARDING
CABIN CREW
COCKPIT
COMFORT
COMMERCIAL
DELTA
DOMESTIC
DRINKS
EMERGENCY
EVACUATION
FLIGHTS
FLYING
FOOD
GALLEY
HAT

HELP
JET
JOB
LUGGAGE
PASSENGERS
PILOTS
PLANES
PURSER
SEAT BELT
SERVICE
SINGLE
TRAINING
UNIFORMS
WINGS
WORK

Flight Attendants

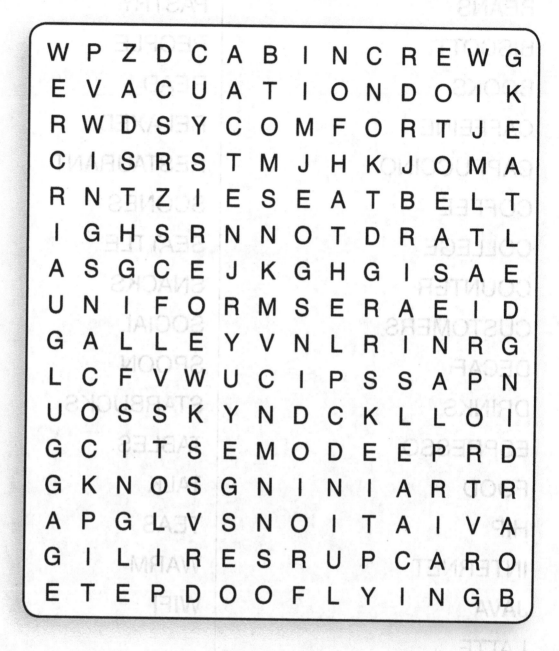

```
W P Z D C A B I N C R E W G
E V A C U A T I O N D O I K
R W D S Y C O M F O R T J E
C I S R S T M J H K J O M A
R N T Z I E S E A T B E L T
I G H S R N N O T D R A T L
A S G C E J K G H G I S A E
U N I F O R M S E R A E I D
G A L L E Y V N L R I N R G
L C F V W U C I P S S A P N
U O S S K Y N D C K L L O I
G C I T S E M O D E E P R D
G K N O S G N I N I A R T R
A P G L V S N O I T A I V A
G I L I R E S R U P C A R O
E T E P D O O F L Y I N G B
```

Solution on Page 327

BARISTA

BEANS

BISCOTTI

BOOKS

CAFFEINE

CAPPUCCINO

COFFEE

COLLEGE

COUNTER

CUSTOMERS

DECAF

DRINKS

ESPRESSO

FOOD

HIP

INTERNET

JAVA

LATTE

MILK

MOCHA

MUFFINS

MUSIC

ORDER

PASTRY

PEOPLE

READ

RELAXED

RESTAURANT

SCONES

SEATTLE

SNACKS

SOCIAL

SPOON

STARBUCKS

TABLES

TALK

TEAS

WARM

WIFI

Coffee Stop

N O O P S E N O C S G M Z B
F E C W L A T T E O G U F Y
T A L K R L S A D F F F A O
O O D P H E T K M R O F C R
S R E M O T S U C O I I E D
S J X Y L E S T D A I N D E
E K A E L I P R A T N S K R
R Q L V C A E H T U K S Z S
P S E M A T I O I C R C B U
S I R O N I C C U P P A C Y
E A W U J S A B O D T F N R
W S O D I H R Y Y S A F W T
I C K B C A K L I M T E A S
F Q X O T E N R E T N I R A
I C M S O T A B L E S N J P
R S N A E B S C O L L E G E

Solution on Page 327

APARTMENTS	MANHATTAN
BAGELS	MONEY
BIG APPLE	MUSEUMS
BOROUGHS	NEW YORK
BROADWAY	RANGERS
BUILDINGS	SHOPPING
BUSINESS	SUBWAYS
CABS	TAXIS
CHEESECAKE	THE BRONX
CITY	THEATRE
CONCERTS	TOURISTS
CRIME	TRAFFIC
CROWDED	URBAN
CULTURE	WALKING
FASHION	
FERRY	
FINANCE	
FOOD	
GOTHAM	
HARLEM	
JETS	
LIGHTS	

Gotham

```
C R I M E K A C E S E E H C
T R A F F I C Y T G L C B O
G O T H A M A N Y N P N W N
P K R O Y W E N E I P A A C
Y F O O D M Z T N D A N L E
T H E A T R E S O L G I K R
X N O R B E H T M I I F I T
Z R A B A G E L S U B H N S
B P H T U R B A N B E M G T
A C A O T O U R I S T S A F
C R R F R A N G E R S X U X
A O L X Y S H O P P I N G M
B W E B U S I N E S S T E J
S D M N O I H S A F E R R Y
A E R U T L U C Y M C I T Y
I D S U B W A Y S T H G I L
```

Solution on Page 327

ASPHALT

BICYCLE

BIKE

BRIDGE

BUS

CARRIAGE

DELIVERY

DRIVER

ENGINE

FOOD

FREIGHT

GOODS

HAULING

HIGHWAYS

LANE

LICENSE

LOAD

LOGS

PAVEMENT

RICKSHAW

ROADS

ROUTE

SCOOTER

SEMI

SIGNS

SPEED

TAXI

TIRES

TOLL ROAD

TRACTOR

TRAFFIC

TRAILER

TRANSPORT

TRAVEL

TRUCKERS

TRUCKING

TURNPIKE

VAN

VEHICLES

WHEELS

Back on the Road

```
C W S E L C I H E V D V L I
V Z P I B B I K E N A L M K
E L E X U L I C E N S E T T
T E E A S P H A L T S T R H
U V D T N E M E V A P R A G
O A W R R O T C A R T U I I
R R U S I O D B I C Y C L E
L T T C D V P O B I F K E R
O W R O S M E S O F M E R F
G A U O D E B R N F G R D H
S H C T O L L R O A D S A E
L S K E O M N R I R R U O N
E K I R G S E R I T L T L G
E C N S O Y R E V I L E D I
H I G H W A Y S N G I S K N
W R I L C M E G D I R B J E
```

Solution on Page 328

ADVENTURE

AMERICA

ANCIENT

ANTARCTICA

ASTRONAUT

CAVE

DE SOTO

DISCOVERY

EXPEDITION

EXPLORERS

FIND

GEOGRAPHY

INFORMATION

JOURNEY

KIRA SALAK

MARCO POLO

MOON

NAVIGATION

NEW WORLD

OCEAN

PORTUGAL

RESEARCH

RESOURCES

SCIENTIFIC

SEARCHING

SHIP

SPAIN

SPECIES

TERRAIN

TRAVELING

UNCOVER

UNKNOWN

Journey of Discovery

```
N T K D P P O T N H N U K A
A E J E A O L U W C A N N O
E R O S C R O A O R V C O L
C R U O I T P N N A I O O S
O A R T R U O O K E G V M E
T I N O E G C R N S A E N C
R N E T M A R T U E T R E R
A O Y K A L A S A R I K W U
V I N F O R M A T I O N W O
E T J S E I C E P S N S O S
L I S C I E N T I F I C R E
I D S E A R C H I N G N L R
N E A P Y R E V O C S I D E
G P E R U T N E V D A A N V
E X P L O R E R S H I P I A
G E O G R A P H Y Y Q S F C
```

Solution on Page 328

AUTOMOBILE

BATTERY

CAR

CHARGING

CLEAN

COMPACT

COST

DRIVING

ECONOMICAL

EFFICIENT

ELECTRIC

EMISSIONS

ENERGY

ENGINE

EXPENSIVE

FRIENDLY

FUTURE

GAS

GREEN

HYBRID

LEAF

LITHIUM

MILEAGE

MOTOR

PLUG IN

POLLUTION

POWER

PRIUS

QUIET

RANGE

RECHARGE

RENEWABLE

SAVINGS

SLOW

SMALL

TECHNOLOGY

VEHICLE

VOLT

WHEELS

Electric Cars

```
X G B G N I V I R D C O S T
L C N M D Y V E H I C L E E
P L F I G C C G R E E N J V
E E A R G H J T S U I R P I
G A E M A R C O M P A C T S
A N L R S E A D I R B Y H N
E Y G O L O N H C E T I K E
L E P E E F F I C I E N T P
I E L I B O M O T U A O A X
M P U B Q S N O I S S I M E
U O G U A O A Y R E T T A B
I W I Q M W Q G F U T U R E
H E N I G N E G N A R L O T
T R C S A V I N G S O L T L
I A W O L S L E E H W O O O
L C A Y L D N E I R F P M V
```

Solution on Page 328

ABU DHABI

BEACHES

BUILDINGS

BURJ

BUSINESS

CAPITAL

CITY

DIVERSE

EXPENSIVE

FAMOUS

FINANCIAL

GOLD

HEAT

HOTELS

KUWAIT

MONARCHY

MUSLIM

NEW

OIL

QATAR

RICH

SAND DUNES

SHEIK

SHOPPING

SULTAN

TOURISTS

TRADE

WATER

WEALTHY

Dubai

```
F F H H Y O I K N P G O T F
F M K S S Q L B E A C H E S
P I I U S K Y L A T I P A C
W L Y L E Z K R A H O X L E
E S E T N X O K C S D A Y Z
K U W A I T P I H Y I U Z L
W M Z N S C R E H C P V B S
F A M O U S I T N D L O G A
U M R V B K L A R S D N H N
B Y H C R A N O M I I S O D
U P O F E I G E L D V V T D
R Z R W F O N L L T E H E U
J A S H O P P I N G R E L N
O S T S I R U O T N S A S E
R E T A W B X R H A E T D S
Y R Y V Q I V W H O J W T E
```

Solution on Page 328

ACCENT	LIVERPOOL
BBC	MONARCHY
BEATLES	OXFORD
CAMBRIDGE	PALACE
CASTLES	PARLIAMENT
CHIPS	PINT
CHURCH	POUND
COUNTRY	PUB
CRICKET	RAIN
CROWN	RUGBY
DIANA	SCOTLAND
EDWARD	SOCCER
ELTON JOHN	STONEHENGE
EMPIRE	TEA
EUROPE	THAMES
FISH	TOURISM
FOOTBALL	UNION JACK
GUARD	WALES
HISTORY	
IRELAND	
ISLAND	
KINGS	

Solution on Page

English Holiday

```
G I S L A N D R A W D E C E
D V E Y T N E M A I L R A P
D R M C R I C K E T I N M O
D I A N A O L C O E V K B R
N T H U U S T N H F E I R U
U O T N G T J S M I R N I E
O U T I Y O C I I S P G D P
P R E O H N I A R H O S G I
Y I C N E H A S E O L E N
B S A J R H B E A T L E S T
G M L A A E S C G A L A N G
U C A C N N A O B U P E N W
R I P K O G T T C B C H S D
E R I P M E O E H C R U H C
D N A L T O C S A S E L A W
J A O X F O R D N W O R C T
```

Solution on Page 329

ASTROS

AUSTIN

BIG

BORDER

CATTLE

COLLEGE

COTTON

COWGIRL

DESERT

EL PASO

FARMING

FOOTBALL

FORT WORTH

GALVESTON

GULF COAST

HEAT

HOUSTON

LARGE

LIVESTOCK

LONE STAR

LONGHORNS

LUBBOCK

MEXICO

OIL

PANHANDLE

PETROLEUM

RANCHES

REFINERIES

RIO GRANDE

RODEO

SOUTH

SPURS

THE ALAMO

UNIVERSITY

The Lone Star State

```
H L R I G W O C A T T L E C
H T G I B L U B B O C K H S
N S R G O E G E L L O C N D
O A D O A G L L A B T O O F
T O M Y W L R I S O R T S A
T C O U T T V A O J D S H R
O F E S E I R E N I F E R M
C L G L A L S O S D A V A I
H U O O D P O R F T E I N N
K G M N R N L R E V O L C G
A M A G E O A E T V C N H H
U E L H D S D H G E I I E T
S X A O R A T E N R P N S U
T I E R O I J A O A A C U O
I C H N B S P U R S P L A S
N O T S U O H D E S E R T W
```

Solution on Page 329

ALPS

ART

BOOT

CATHOLIC

CHEESE

COUNTRY

CUISINE

CULTURE

DA VINCI

DANTE

EUROPE

FAMILY

FASHION

FERRARI

FLAG

FLORENCE

FOOD

GALILEO

GELATO

HISTORY

ITALIANS

LANGUAGE

LASAGNA

LATIN

MAFIA

MILAN

MUSEUMS

NAPLES

PASTA

PISA

PIZZA

POPE

ROMANTIC

RUINS

SICILY

TOURISM

TRAVEL

TUSCANY

VENICE

WINE

Italian Tour

```
J I R A R R E F A M I L Y V
F O O D Q Y R O T S I H P E
R S M U E S U M O L A T I N
M L E V A R T O E F L A G I
E I W I N E L J E S E E H C
P B L E G A U G N A L X C E
O O F A S X C A A A W A M E
R O M A N T I C T T T S F T
U T G D S L C O C H I L U N
E N A R A H J U O R O S O A
A R S T B V I L U R C I K D
Y L I C I S I O E A I F A M
P O P E I C T N N A P L E S
Y R T N U O C Y C A T S A P
W N E H B E O E L I L A G L
K N A Z Z I P R U I N S S A
```

Solution on Page 329

ALBUM

APERTURE

ART

BEAUTY

CAMERA

CAPTURE

COLORS

COMPUTER

DARKROOM

DEVELOP

DIGITAL

DOCUMENT

EVENT

EXPOSURE

FACE

FILM

FLASH

FOCUS

FRAME

HISTORY

IMAGES

LENS

LIGHT

MODEL

NATURE

NEGATIVE

PANORAMIC

PAPER

PEOPLE

PHOTO

PICTURES

PORTRAIT

POSING

PRINTING

RECORD

SCENE

SENSOR

SHARE

SLIDE

STILL

Take Pictures

```
S H A R E M A R F D J D F V
L C O L O R S K I O E A R T
I R A C B M E G K V C P P S
D R E P B U I T E E T U O T
E E V P E T M L U I N Z S I
L C I M A R O N A P E M I L
E O T L U P T R G S M O N L
N R A I T K T U E C U O G E
S D G F Y R J R R U C R C D
O I E Q O R U Y U E O K A O
P M N P O T R U S N D R P M
F A I S C O T L O A Y A T E
L G N I T N I R P T R D U N
A E P S E G V A X U O B R E
S S I V H C A M E R A H E C
H H E T Q E L P O E P L P S
```

Solution on Page 329

ADVENTURES

BAMBOO

BEACH

BOAT

BOB DENVER

CAPTAIN

CASTAWAYS

CLASSIC

COCONUT

COMEDY

CRUISE

GILLIGAN

GINGER

HAMMOCK

HOWELLS

ISLAND

LAGOON

LOST

LOVEY

MARY ANN

MOVIE STAR

MR. HOWELL

OCEAN

PROFESSOR

RADIO

RESCUE

SHIPWRECK

SITCOM

SKIPPER

STORM

STRANDED

TELEVISION

THE MINNOW

THEME SONG

TOUR

TROPICAL

TV SHOW

Stuck on Gilligan's Island

```
O C E A N I A T P A C V S E
L A C I P O R T A O B H K U
C M Q Q S H I P W R E C K C
Y A G C S C A S T A W A Y S
D R D I L T R M I O B E P E
E Y H V L A H U M V U B R R
M A E Q E L S E I O E R O M
O N Y V W N I S M S C L F R
C N S M O W T G I I E K E O
O O T O H L O U A C N V S T
C O R C R O R H R N N N S S
O G A T M R A T S E I V O M
N A N I S L A N D V S T R W
U L D S B A M B O O T S O L
T H E M E S O N G I N G E R
O I D A R B S K I P P E R F
```

Solution on Page 330

ALCOHOL

ALTBIER

AMBER ALE

AMERICAN

AROMA

ASSYRIAN

BELGIAN

BOCK

BREWED

BROWN ALE

CHAMPAGNE

CIDER

COLOR

CREAM ALE

DARK

DUNKEL

FRUIT

GERMAN

GRAINS

GRAVITY

HEAD

HOPS

IPA

LAGERS

LAMBIC

LIGHT

MALT

MOUTHFEEL

OLD ALE

PALE ALE

PILSNER

PORTER

RED ALE

RYE BEER

SPICED

STRENGTH

SWEETNESS

VISCOSITY

WATER

YEAST

Beers Around the World

```
S P O H F I N A M R E G J M
P K W G R A I N S V N A E A
I T C I B M A L I S G L E L
C I D E R I P S R R A T L T
E U S E G I C E A N P B A S
D R S L L O G V W C M I D A
E F E S S A I O A O A E E E
W B N I L T R W P L H R R Y
E E T A Y B A E V O C B E R
R Y E M I K C O B R R R E A
B L E E F H T U O M E T B M
T H W R K I P A L E A L E O
H N S I R D A E H W M W Y R
G T R C A S S Y R I A N R A
I E L A D L O H O C L A Q D
L E K N U D H T G N E R T S
```

Solution on Page 330

AEROSTAT

AIRCRAFT

AIRPLANE

AIRPORT

AKRON

AVIATION

BALLOON

BLIMPS

BUOYANT

CRASH

DIRIGIBLES

ENGINE

FLIGHT

FLOAT

FUEL

GAS

GERMANY

GONDOLA

HINDENBURG

HISTORY

HOT AIR

HYDROGEN

LANDING

LIFT

PASSENGERS

PILOT

PROPELLERS

RESEARCH

SKY

TECHNOLOGY

THRUST

TURBULENCE

UNPOWERED

WINGS

ZEPPELINS

```
G O N D O L A E N I G N E Z
E L I F T H I S T O R Y Q E
R N S Y G O L O N H C E T P
M E A P M R A I R P O R T P
A G M L M F U H S A R C R E
N O V N P I U B B S F O E L
Y R A O O R L E N S P K W I
U D I R I G I B L E S G D N
T Y R K E C E A L N D E A S
A H C A W S F L O G R N V S
T U R B U L E N C E I O I T
S W A U O R T A W R A O A H
O I F A S O T O R S T L T G
R N T U L T P N S C O L I I
E G N I D N A L K N H A O L
A S P T U T N A Y O U B N F
```

Solution on Page 330

AIR

AXLE

BICYCLE

BIKE

BMX

BOLTS

BRAKES

DIAMETER

DROPOUTS

FAST

FORK

FRAME

GEARS

INFLATE

LACING

LOCK

METAL

MOUNTAIN

NUT

PARTS

PATCH

PEDAL

PRESSURE

RACING

RIDING

RIMS

ROAD

ROLLING

ROTATING

ROUND

RUBBER

SEAT

SPEED

SPOKES

SPROCKET

SUPPORT

TRACTION

TREAD

VALVE

WRENCH

Bicycle Wheels

```
B I K E L Q S V D D G F R N
K C O L J T H L G B R P I T
B U S X R C A N R A R A A D
V I U A T D I A M E T E R F
X X P A E L K E S N S O A R
B M P P L E D S U S P S C Z
Q B O O S A U O G O T T I R
C O R T O R M K U N V U N U
A L T R E R O T A T I N G B
A T A A C K S R O U N D L B
H S F C E L C Y C I B A I E
W D O T I I D O G B T N G R
Z A R I K N J W R E N C H I
S E K O P S G I M P A R O M
H R I N F L A T E A S R S S
M T V A L V E M D E E P S M
```

Solution on Page 330

ANTEATER	PHARMACY
BANANAS	PIRANHA
BANYAN	PORCUPINES
BASILISK	PROTECTED
BINTURONG	RHINOCEROS
CASSOWARY	SLOTH
CLEARING	TAPIRS
COATI	TEMPERATE
COBRA	TERMITES
COCKATOO	VINES
CROCODILES	
FERNS	
FLYING FOX	
GIBBON	
JAGUARS	
KAKAPO	
KINKAJOU	
LEMUR	
MACHETE	
MANIOC	
MONSOON	
OKAPIS	

Solution on

Jungle Journey

```
A H T O L S B S R A U G A J
H O R U O J A K N I K S R M
N Q T C O I N A M R S I B P
A W E O T B A N Y A N P O H
R K R A A V N R S R R A C A
I S M T K M A S E E E K H R
P I I I C W S E L W F O B M
R L T X O F G N I Y L F I A
O I E S C I A I D P T M N C
T S S E B G N P O S A A T Y
E A Z B B O T U C E P C U O
C B O S O R E C O N I H R P
T N P S U C A R R I R E O A
E L N M M F T O C V S T N K
D O E T A R E P M E T E G A
M L X G N I R A E L C A K K
```

Solution on Page 331

ACURA	MONEY
AUDI	PLEASANT
BENTLEY	PORSCHE
BMW	PREMIUM
BRAND	PRESTIGE
CADILLAC	RICH
CLASS	RIDE
COMFORT	RIMS
DESIRABLE	SEDAN
EXPENSIVE	SMOOTH
FAST	SPACE
FEATURES	STATUS
FERRARI	STYLE
INFINITI	SUNROOF
JAGUAR	SUPERIOR
LARGE	TOWN CAR
LEATHER	VALUE
LEXUS	WEALTHY
LIMOUSINE	
LINCOLN	
LUXURY	
MERCEDES	

Luxury Vehicles

```
E C L S I S T A T U S M I R
D F A E N V E R E H T A E L
I W C D F J A G U A R S J S
R Q O A I C R O I R E P U S
F F M N N L E L Y T S A F A
M O F W I Z L E X U S C E L
W E O O T N B A S F R E R C
E T R R I L A E C L V S R I
A W T C N P R E M I U M A P
L A R G E U I A S M N O R O
T U D V T D S N R O L O I R
H D N A R B E T I U O T M S
Y I E L I P D S C S C H O C
H F L U X U R Y H I N A N H
W M B E N T L E Y N I F E E
B F A S T N A S A E L P Y X
```

Solution on Page 331

AIR

BATHROOM

BREAK

CAMP

CARS

COFFEE

DIRECTIONS

DRIVER

EAT

EXPRESSWAY

FOOD

FREEWAY

GAS

HIGHWAY

INTERSTATE

MAPS

PARKING

PASSENGER

PICNIC

PLAZA

PUBLIC

REFUEL

REST STOP

RESTAURANT

RESTROOMS

ROAD

SCENIC

SERVICE

STRETCH

TABLES

TOILETS

TOURIST

TRAVELERS

TRUCKERS

TURNPIKE

VENDING

WATER

Rest Areas

```
T O I L E T S K Y I D O O F
O G A S E L B A T H R O O M
U N R E T A W O R M I D H S
R I O P A E S E A X V I C P
I D A A E T S T V C E R T U
S N D R C N M A E A R E E B
T E F K I A O T L M X C R L
R V G I V R O S E P T T T I
E S H N R U R R C P I S C
F C I G E A T E S O O O P I
U E G B S T S T P F T N L N
E N H R Y S E N A F S S A C
L I W E W E R I M E T R Z I
I C A A I R E G N E S S A P
I J Y K Z T R U C K E R S C
F F L N F E K I P N R U T L
```

Solution on Page 331

BARGE

BOATS

CANALS

CARRIER

COMMERCE

CONTAINERS

CREW

CRUISE

DECK

DOCKS

DREDGER

EXPORT

FERRIES

FREIGHT

GOODS

HARBOR

HOLD

HULL

IMPORT

INVENTORY

LINER

LOAD

MARINERS

MERCHANT

MILITARY

OCEAN

PACIFIC

PASSENGERS

PORTS

RECREATION

RIVERS

ROPE

SAILBOAT

SEA

SHIPPING

TANKERS

TRAVEL

TUGBOAT

WATERCRAFT

On a Ship

```
T  H  N  D  H  O  L  D  Y  R  O  P  E  S
J  M  A  R  E  I  R  R  A  C  S  G  S  D
X  E  P  R  N  C  O  T  M  V  R  C  C  O
G  R  S  E  B  T  K  A  H  A  E  O  E  O
N  C  R  S  N  O  S  O  B  G  N  M  X  G
I  H  E  E  O  R  R  B  W  T  I  M  P  A
P  A  V  I  I  E  L  A  A  R  E  O  G
P  N  I  R  T  G  G  I  T  N  A  R  R  C
I  T  R  R  A  D  N  A  E  K  M  C  T  F
H  U  L  E  E  E  E  S  R  E  W  E  R  C
S  G  E  F  R  R  S  C  C  R  U  I  S  E
L  B  V  S  C  D  S  D  R  S  K  C  O  D
A  O  A  T  E  T  A  P  A  C  I  F  I  C
N  A  R  A  R  O  P  R  F  O  C  E  A  N
A  T  T  O  L  Y  R  A  T  I  L  I  M  U
C  L  P  B  I  M  P  O  R  T  H  U  L  L
```

Solution on Page 331

ASIAN

BANGKOK

BHUTAN

BUDDHISM

BURMA

CAMBODIA

CHINA

COUNTRY

CUISINE

CULTURE

EASTERN

ECONOMY

EURASIA

GEOGRAPHY

HINDUISM

HONG KONG

INDONESIA

ISLAM

JAPAN

LANGUAGES

LAOS

LARGE

MALAYSIA

MONGOLIA

MYANMAR

NEPAL

ORIENTAL

PAKISTAN

PEOPLE

POPULOUS

RUSSIA

SINGAPORE

SRI LANKA

TAIWAN

TEA

THAILAND

VIETNAM

Solution on pg. 34

Around Asia

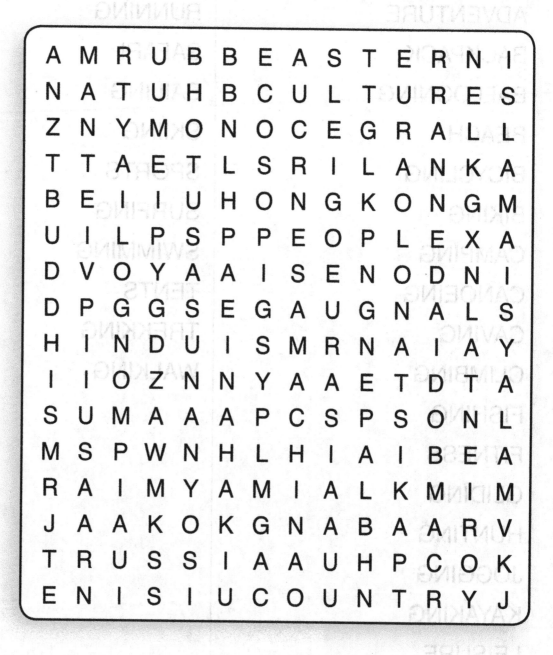

```
A M R U B B E A S T E R N I
N A T U H B C U L T U R E S
Z N Y M O N O C E G R A L L
T T A E T L S R I L A N K A
B E I I U H O N G K O N G M
U I L P S P P E O P L E X A
D V O Y A A I S E N O D N I
D P G G S E G A U G N A L S
H I N D U I S M R N A I A Y
I I O Z N N Y A A E T D T A
S U M A A A P C S P S O N L
M S P W N H L H I A I B E A
R A I M Y A M I A L K M I M
J A A K O K G N A B A A R V
T R U S S I A A U H P C O K
E N I S I U C O U N T R Y J
```

Solution on Page 332

ACTIVITIES
ADVENTURE
BACKPACK
BALLOONING
BEACH
BICYCLING
BIKING
CAMPING
CANOEING
CAVING
CLIMBING
FISHING
FITNESS
GLIDING
HUNTING
JOGGING
KAYAKING
LEISURE
MOUNTAINS
NATURE
PARK
RACING

RAFTING
RUNNING
SAFARI
SAILING
SKIING
SPORTS
SURFING
SWIMMING
TENTS
TREKKING
WALKING

Outdoor Recreation

```
G R A Z G N I C A R A S O R
G U S C P C R A F T I N G S
N N K S T L G N I M M I W S
I N I G N I N O O L L A B G
T I I H T M V E E R U T A N
N N N W S B F I T G A N C I
U G G T Z I G N T N D U K K
H D N N T N F G G I V O P L
G E L N I G P N N L E M A A
T N E D F P I I I C N S C W
G S I X S K M K V Y T A K G
S L S G K A R A A C U I H N
G V U E G A F Y C I R L C I
S P R X P O Q A T B E I A K
F T E M K B J K R Y X N E I
S P O R T S U R F I N G B B
```

Solution on Page 332

AIRPORT

CHATTAHOOCHEE

CITY

CIVIL WAR

CNN

COCA-COLA

ENTERTAINMENT

FULTON COUNTY

HARTSFIELD

HISTORICAL

HOME DEPOT

HUB

LARGE

METROPOLITAN

MODERN

PEACHTREE

PHILIPS ARENA

PIEDMONT PARK

SKYSCRAPERS

SPORTS

TED TURNER

THRASHERS

TOURISM

TRAVEL

TURNER FIELD

UNDERGROUND

UNITED STATES

URBAN

USA

```
D N U O R G R E D N U G Y L
Y A A N S R E H S A R H T S
H T P L I M O D E R N O N K
T I N H O T O U R I S M E Y
E L S U I C E L A R G E M S
D O C T O L A D B U H D N C
T P I A O C I C S P E I R
U O V I S R N P O T N P A A
R R I R P N I O S C A O T P
N T L P O A H C T A B T R E
E E W O R A U S A L R X E R
R M A R T R A V E L U E T S
H A R T S F I E L D O F N D
K R A P T N O M D E I P E A
R H D L E I F R E N R U T I
C I T Y P E A C H T R E E G
```

Solution on Page 332

BARGE	RAFT
BOW	RECREATION
CABIN	RIVER
CANOE	ROW
CREW	SAILBOAT
CRUISE	SAILING
DECKS	SEA
ENGINE	SHIP
FERRYBOAT	SKI
FIBERGLASS	STARBOARD
FISHING	STERN
FLOAT	SUN
HULL	TRAVEL
KAYAK	TRIP
KEEL	WATER
LAKE	WHEEL
LIFEBOAT	WOODEN
MOTOR	YACHT
NAUTICAL	
OCEAN	
PADDLES	
PORT	

Solution on Page

Watercraft

```
O E G T M C F S I A Q I N Z
W G N D E C K S O P E K H M
T N T I R G N I L I A S D W
R I R U G P L A C I T U A N
A H I E I N E O N A C W N O
V S P H T F E R R Y B O A T
E I S R L S K B R O I S U A
L F O A M I O V D T E A R O
N P H O L A F D A L T I D L
W A T E R G O E D S F L A F
W O O D E N R D B C A B I N
R E L B N C A E L O R O K U
O H E A E P M C B O A A L S
W G E R E V I R W I Y T L R
P C H G L A K E N A F Y U Q
O M W E R B O W K Y A C H T
```

Solution on Page 332

ALPS

AMSTERDAM

ANCIENT

AUSTRIA

BELGIUM

BERLIN

BLACK SEA

BORDERS

CITIES

CONTINENT

COUNTRIES

CURRENCY

DENMARK

ENGLAND

EURASIA

FINLAND

FRANCE

GERMANY

HISTORY

ICELAND

IRELAND

ITALY

KINGS

LANGUAGES

LONDON

LUXEMBOURG

MONARCHY

NATO

PARIS

POLAND

PORTUGAL

SCOTLAND

SERBIA

SPAIN

VATICAN

Around Europe

```
Z S E I T I C E L A N D M V
S N A C I T A V C K I N G S
G E R M A N Y B O R D E R S
Y H U S C O T L A N D S U D
H Q N R S D N A L N I F O N
C R I P A A E S K C A L B A
R U L C T S N I A P S L M L
A A R O O A I R T S U A E E
N E E R I U T A Y I D G X R
O N B T E N N R S R P U U I
M G A E E N O T E A T T L E
B L Y I L T C T R P H R O C
Y A C B S G S Y B I N O N N
H N J I E M I C I K E P D A
A D H L A N G U A G E S O R
P O L A N D E N M A R K N F
```

Solution on Page 333

AMERICA

BASKETBALL

BLACKHAWKS

BLUES

BUILDINGS

BULLS

BUSINESS

CARS

COLD

CRIME

DALEY

FIRE

FOOTBALL

HOT DOG

ILLINOIS

INDUSTRY

JAZZ

JORDAN

LAKEFRONT

LIGHTS

MIDWEST

MUSICAL

NAVY PIER

PIZZA

POLITICS

SNOW

THE LOOP

TOURISM

TRAFFIC

TRIBUNE

UNIVERSITY

URBAN

WHITE SOX

WINDY CITY

The Windy City

```
M I D W E S T O U R I S M W
L I G H T S R A C Y J A Z Z
W O N S Q E W H I T E S O X
Z S S S G N I D L I U B L C
L E N U B I R T I S E A L I
L U A C E S B Y K R K N A F
A L M R L U M W D E A F B F
B B E I A B A P F V W G T A
T U R M L H O R Y I G O O R
E L I E K L O P N N F D O T
K L C C I N I D L U I T F D
S S A T T E Y N A D R O J A
A L I C R C P O O L E H T L
B C O E I K L A C I S U M E
S L E T D R I N D U S T R Y
D J Y A Z Z I P N A B R U Z
```

Solution on Page 333

ALOHA

AMERICA

CLIMATE

COCONUT

COFFEE

CULTURE

HISTORY

HONOLULU

HOTEL

HUMID

ISLANDS

KAUAI

LAVA

LUAU

MAUI

MOUNTAIN

OAHU

OBAMA

PINEAPPLE

POLYNESIAN

RAINBOW

RESORTS

SAND

SEA

SUGARCANE

SUNSET

SURFING

TOURISTS

TRAVEL

TROPICS

USA

VOLCANOES

WATER

WAVES

```
A V L E T O H M Z A P G R U
M W A V E S O Z L U I U A M
A W A L S U C O C O N U T R
B O E S N Q L W A T E R H I
O B T T U E N A C R A G U S
G N A I S E N Y L O P M A L
J I M Q E U T K U S P A A A
N A I W O I A O A J L M S N
H R L L N U W N U O E C I D
U I C K A L D L H R I I C S
M T S I C V U A I P I W U E
I N R T L L A C O N H S L Q
D U H A O I A R E S O R T S
N S E N V R T G N I F R U S
A S O Z S E Y R O U U Z R J
R H Y H Y I L C O F F E E N
```

Solution on Page 333

BOSTON	REVOLUTION
BRITAIN	SALEM
BRITISH	SETTLEMENT
COLONIES	SPAIN
CONGRESS	TAXATION
COTTON	TEA
DELAWARE	THIRTEEN
DEMOCRACY	TRADE
DUTCH	VIRGINIA
ENGLAND	WASHINGTON
FRANKLIN	
FREEDOM	
GOVERNMENT	
JAMESTOWN	
KING	
MARYLAND	
MAYFLOWER	
NEW YORK	
PILGRIMS	
PLYMOUTH	
PURITANS	
RELIGION	

Colonial Tour

```
K Y S D O N I L K N A R F B
A R C N U S W Z C E M G C R
I E O A A T N O T S O B O I
N N N Y R T C E T V D G T T
I G G I W C I H E S E N T I
G L R N A E O R X T E O O S
R A E O V P N M U M R M N H
I N S T A M S G E P F I A T
V D S G E E N L L D K S H J
B E V N O I T U L O V E R T
R L T I K T R E L I G I O N
I A R H E M A R Y L A N D M
T W A S M I R G L I P O B E
A A D A G H T U O M Y L P L
I R E W O L F Y A M Q O F A
N E T A X A T I O N Y C M S
```

Solution on Page 333

ANIMALS	HOMESTEAD
AREA	HORSES
BEEF	LANDSCAPE
BISON	LIVESTOCK
BRANDING	MEAT
BULLS	PASTURE
CALF	PRAIRIE
CATTLE	RANCHING
CORRAL	RIDE
COUNTRY	RODEO
COWBOYS	ROPE
COWHAND	SADDLE
CROPS	SHEEP
DUDE	SOUTH
EMU	STEER
FARMERS	TEXAS
FARMING	WESTERN
FENCES	WOOL
FIELD	
GRAZING	
HAY	
HERD	

Dude Ranch

```
R E E T S L O E L D D A S K
C C R O P S O C A T T L E E
S A X E T R C O O Z E E S U
A L N A A E O W W U G P R Q
G F G I E M R B E B N L O T
H N N O M R R O S J I T H R
O J I E L A A Y T V H G R T
B I Z D A F L S E K C G D Y
E E A O N E P S R I N N L A
E I R R D A T K N N A I E X
F R G U S O R Y A H R M I V
E I D T C S I B W B P R F X
N A U K A O J O U I E A A R
C R S M P U C D X S E F L I
E P D A E T S E M O H E R D
S L L U B H N G E N S X B E
```

Solution on Page 334

ARCH

ATOLL

BASIN

BAYOU

BEACH

BUTTE

CANYON

CAPE

CAVE

CLIFF

COVE

CRATER

DELTA

DESERT

DUNE

FIELD

FJORD

FLUVIAL

GLACIER

GULLY

HILL

ISLAND

ISTHMUS

MARSH

MESA

OASIS

PLATEAU

RANGE

RAVINE

REEF

RIDGE

RIVER

ROCK

SEA

SLOPE

SOIL

SOUND

SWAMP

VALLEY

VOLCANO

Landforms along the Way

```
Y G P U C C B E P O L S U X
S A Q T R A X D H E I D A F
O M H O K P M A W S G Z D H
U K C J J E M E A H R D C N
N K R B N Y C O G K U A I S
D K A I I O L D F N E S M R
R C C G V S M L E B A Y O U
O B D E L E T T U B T R X F
J D U N S A R H O G O G F E
F S E A A U C N M X L I T E
F I O L J L A I V U L F R R
K X E I T C S E E C S E E V
C Y E L L A V I T R T V S I
R A L O D N O Y N A C A E S
M I V E N I V A R U L C D S
H W T U M O H C Z C P P W E
```

Solution on Page 334

BALANCE

BRISK

COMMUTE

DISTANCE

DOG

EXERCISE

FEET

FITNESS

FOOTPATH

FUN

GAIT

GROUND

HEALTHY

HIKING

JOGGING

KNEES

LEGS

LEISURE

MALL

MARCHING

MILES

MOVEMENT

MUSCLES

NATURE

PACE

POWER

ROAD

RUNNING

SIDEWALK

SLOW

SPEED

STEPS

STICK

STRENGTH

STRIDE

TRAILS

TRAVEL

WATER

WELLNESS

WORKOUT

```
E T U M M O C S T I C K S I
R I S O L L A M T O K G F H
U A T V G R O U N D E N E S
S G R E P E C N A L A B E H
I E E M G E C A P T T L T R
E C N E N F U N U R I A K O
L C G N I H C R A M P S L A
G F T T G E E V S T I E A D
N S H U G A E P O R S I W W
I L I O O L E O B I D I E A
N O K K J T F R C E P L D T
N W I R S H J R E Q L G I E
U F N O A Y E P K N E E S R
R J G W V X S S E N T I F S
N P O W E R C S E L C S U M
X E D I R T S L I A R T A F
```

Solution on Page 334

AGRICULTURE

BADGER STATE

BEER

BREWERS

BUCKS

CHEESEHEADS

CHIPPEWA

COLD

CORN

DAIRYLAND

DOOR COUNTY

FARMING

FOOTBALL

GREAT LAKES

ICE FISHING

KENOSHA

LAKE MICHIGAN

LAKE SUPERIOR

LAMBEAU FIELD

NORTHERN

PAPER MILLS

RIVERS

ROBIN

SKIING

SNOW

SPORTS

SUGAR MAPLE

SUMMERFEST

UNIVERSITY

```
U N I V E R S I T Y G L Y S
D B R E W E R S T R A N U P
N O R T H E R N E K I M F O
A D L E I F U A E B M A L R
L C Y H I O T M O E R Y E T
Y O U B C L I R R M E E S S
R L B R A C O F I R B D L U
I D O K H D E N U A A L S G
A O E I K S G T W E I K R A
D S G Y T S L E H M I N E R
L A K E S U P E R I O R V M
N W A K C P S E N S M O I A
I P C I I E P G V W T C R P
U U R H E A F O O T B A L L
B G C H P K E N O S H A T E
A I C E F I S H I N G X G E
```

Solution on Page 334

AFRICA

AMERICAS

ANTARCTICA

AREAS

ATLAS

AUSTRALIA

BORDERS

BOUNDARY

CITIES

CONTINUOUS

CONVENTION

COUNTRY

DIVISIONS

DRIFT

EURASIA

GEOGRAPHY

GEOLOGICAL

GREENLAND

INDIA

ISLAND

LANDMASSES

MAINLAND

MOUNTAINS

NORTH AMERICA

OCEANS

POPULATION

REGIONS

SEPARATION

SHELF

SOUTH AMERICA

WORLD

Continents

```
A Q V B O U N D A R Y B F D
T T F I R D N A L N I A M N
L T E F C R E G I O N S J A
A G E O L O G I C A L N N L
S C L N C O N T I N U O U S
M Y I A O S J V O C R I S I
O H A R N I Y I E T A S N L
U P I I F D T R H N H I A G
N A D A S A M A T E T V E R
T R N B R A M A L N T I C E
A G I A D E R F S U U D O E
I O P N R C A U D S P O T N
N E C I T I E S E L E O C L
S G C I J B O R D E R S P A
X A C I R E M A H T U O S N
S A U S T R A L I A B F W D
```

Solution on Page 335

BOXCAR

CARS

COAL

CONTAINER

CONVEYANCE

CROSSINGS

DIESEL

DINING CAR

ELECTRICAL

ENGINES

FREIGHT

GOODS

HAUL

LINE

LOCOMOTIVE

MONORAIL

MOVEMENT

PASSENGERS

PEOPLE

PLATFORM

RAILROADS

RAILWAY

ROUTE

SHIPPING

SLEEPERS

STATION

STEEL

STOPS

SWITCHES

TICKET

TIES

TRACKS

TRAINS

TRANSPORT

TRAVEL

WHISTLE

```
T W S T A T I O N C T R E L
I H Y A W L I A R R E T S U
C I G O O D S O A N U R T A
K S L I N E S I I O T A E H
E T T I E S L A R N H N E T
T L A C I R T C E L E S L R
R E I N O N F M R S R P O A
A A G A O N E U E L A O C V
C S D C R V V H Y S C R O E
K S S D O O C E S S G T M L
S E P M I T N E Y R N B O P
N N O H I E N O D A I O T O
I I T W N G S U M C N X I E
A G S L E E P E R S I C V P
R N M R O F T A L P D A E K
T E S H I P P I N G N R X R
```

Solution on Page 335

ACADIAN	NEW ENGLAND
AMERICAN	PAULA DEEN
APPLES	PIZZA
BAKED BEANS	POTATOES
BARBECUE	REGIONAL
BEER	RESTAURANTS
CAJUN	SANDWICH
CLAMBAKE	SEAFOOD
COLONIAL	SOUL FOOD
COOKING	SOUTHERN
CORN	TEX MEX
CREOLE	TURKEY
EMERIL	WINE
ETHNIC	
FAST FOOD	
FATS	
FRUITS	
GRILLING	
HAMBURGERS	
HOT DOGS	
LOBSTER	
LOUISIANA	

Cuisine Across the U.S.

```
D O O F A E S T I U R F P A
S N A E B D E K A B M A L C
A U A M N N R E H T U O S A
N T D L E I S O U L F O O D
D H E O G R W G A Z Z I P I
W A B X O N I D O R E E B A
I M A R M F E C N D L C L N
C B R E L E T W A O T A J S
H U B T N O X S E N I O J N
C R E S T A U R A N T S H U
I G C B U N C I O F A T S J
N E U O R R A L S E L P P A
H R E L K C O O K I N G R C
T S O G E C S E O T A T O P
E R C C Y G R I L L I N G U
L I R E M E R E G I O N A L
```

Solution on Page 335

ARABS

ARCHITECTURE

ARID CLIMATE

BEACHES

BUILDINGS

CAPITAL

CITY

CONSTRUCTION

COSMOPOLITAN

CUISINE

CULTURE

DESERT

DIVERSE

DUBAI

EMIRATES PALACE

ETIHAD AIRWAYS

ETISALAT

GOVERNMENT

METROPOLIS

MIDDLE EAST

OIL

PERSIAN GULF

PORT

REAL ESTATE

REEM ISLAND

RICH

SALAM STREET

SAND

SKYSCRAPERS

UAE

WEALTHY

Abu Dhabi

```
A Y S K Y S C R A P E R S S
M R C S I L O P O R T E M B
I Z C I E T I S A L A T N A
D C Y H T L A E W I T U O R
D O A L I Y T M C O S T I A
L S R T H T E M A U E S T P
E M I R A T E S P A L A C E
E O D E D N R C I E A N U R
A P C E A E T U T R E D R S
S O L M I M S I A U R I T I
T L I I R N M S L T R V S A
R I M S W R A I R L D E N N
E T A L A E L N I U U R O G
S A T A Y V A E C C B S C U
E N E N S O S E H C A E B L
D L Q D S G N I D L I U B F
```

Solution on Page 335

BUS STOP

CHARTER

CITY BUS

COACH

COMMUTE

DIESEL

DOORS

DRIVER

ENGINE

FARE

LONG

METRO

MINI

PASSENGERS

PEOPLE

PRIVATE

RAIL

RIDE

ROUTES

SCHOOL BUS

SEATS

SERVICE

SIT

STATION

STOPS

TICKET

TOUR

TRANSFER

TRAVEL

TROLLEY

VEHICLE

WINDOW

YELLOW

```
L E V A R T G E K S B U H P
V D S T A E S S E R V I C E
O I G E P G V E W S S O A L
E R S U B Y T I C E M C O C
L F A R E P N H R M E T C I
M D N L X D O E U D I C K H
H O L P O O T T A S H N T E
Y O K W L A E E S A M R I V
W R Z B V Y N H R S E A C D
E S U I D I Y T L F U S K I
K S R E G N E S S A P B E E
V P K N M R S N O I T A T S
K W E R W E A X P E O P L E
Y E L L O R T I I Q U U O L
J R O U T E S R L X R E N P
A J O Z C R S P O T S H G O
```

AIR	NATURAL
ANIMALS	OCEANS
BEAUTY	OUTSIDE
BIOLOGY	PLANTS
CLIMATE	POND
CLOUDS	RAIN
DESERT	RIVERS
EARTH	ROCKS
ECOLOGY	SKY
FAUNA	SNOW
FIELD	SOIL
FISH	STREAMS
FLORA	SUN
FORESTS	TREES
GEOLOGY	WATER
GRASS	WEATHER
GREEN	WILDLIFE
HUMAN	WIND
LAKES	
LAND	
LEAVES	
MOTHER	

```
U V H I S S N U S N A E C O
A R T K E Y Z D C J K A A W
I I R V K G U B L P W N R Q
R V A V A O K Y I O I U O H
P E E J L L G G M M L A L S
L R H C D O J O A B D F F I
Y S I T L E G L T D L E I F
W O G O A G S O E L I O S T
S M C S R E B I S Q F U Z R
N E P I U R W B T O E H Q E
O D V L T A W D R D B U S E
W I D A A I A E E E Q M G S
A S Z N N N S M A S S A R G
T T Y D O T T U M E W N E L
E U J K S P T S S R N R E Q
R O C K S Y R E H T O M N X
```

Solution on Page 336

AIRCRAFT

AUTOMOBILE

BICYCLES

BIKE

BOATS

BUS

CART

DRIVE

ELECTRIC

ENGINE

FORD

GAS

HELICOPTER

HOVERCRAFT

LAND

LICENSE

MECHANIC

MOTORCYCLE

OIL

PASSENGER

PEOPLE

PLANE

POWER

ROAD

ROCKET

SCOOTER

SEDAN

SHIPS

SPACECRAFT

STEERING

TRAINS

TRANSPORT

TRAVEL

TRUCK

VAN

WATER

WHEELED

YACHT

Vehicles

```
E T G A S P Q S A D R I V E
N T E T U S E I E O N C A N
I R C L N T R O C D I E N A
G V B I C C O K P N A S T L
N N A C R Y E M A L H N F P
E R I A P T C H O T E E A Y
T D F R S O C R K B L C R A
Z T L T E E W E O B I I C C
S R A I M E M E L T C L R H
U O S C O O T E R E O I E T
B P R E G N E S S A P M V S
I S P A C E C R A F T R O S
K N W F B I C Y C L E S H L
E A W H E E L E D T R I A M
T R A V E L R O A D P N Z C
V T R U C K Z W S S D R O F
```

Solution on Page 336

AIRFARE

AIRLINES

ATTENDANTS

CARRYON

COACH

CONCOURSE

CUSTOMS

ELEVATORS

ESCALATORS

FUSELAGE

GATE

GIFT SHOP

JET

KITTY HAWK

LAX

MECHANICS

NAVIGATORS

NYC

OVERHEAD

PILOTS

PROPELLER

RESTAURANT

RUDDER

RUNWAY

SKYCAPS

TAKEOFF

TAXI

WALKWAY

WINGS

Around the Airport

```
U H T E Y A W N U R V K E K
E C W X B P O X T P L T A N
I Y E A S F F O E K A T A H
A I R L I N E S J G T V C F
P R O P E L L E R E I A O M
N D Q M K V A F N G O C N A
O S G N I W A D A C K U C G
Y E S C A L A T O R S S O D
R W C F P N O H O K Q T U A
R A I U T R O S Y R X O R E
A L N S S P I L O T S M S H
C K A E T N A R U A T S E R
Y W H L X P O H S T F I G E
N A C A I R F A R E A W K V
T Y E G S P A C Y K S X C O
X M M E R E D D U R K T I R
```

Solution on Page 336

ALPS

BANKING

BERN

CANTONS

CHEESE

CHOCOLATE

COLD

COUNTRY

EUROPEAN

FONDUE

FRANC

FRENCH

FUN

GENEVA

GERMANY

GLACIERS

HEIDI

ITALIAN

LANDLOCKED

LUCERNE

MATTERHORN

MOUNTAINS

NATION

NEUTRALITY

PARLIAMENT

RED CROSS

REPUBLIC

SKIING

SNOW

SWISS

TOURISTS

TRAVEL

VALLEYS

WATCHES

WEALTH

WINE

YODELING

Switzerland

```
X S S Y N A L P S Q F W D N
M E S N R L U C E R N E W S
C H O C O L A T E O K U E S
I C R N H W C N R C R R A K
L T C E R E C O O A T O L I
B A D U E H E L L P V P T I
U W E T T Y D S I D I E H N
P Y R R T N S R E I C A L G
E K I A A Y J S W I N E N
R S T L M O U N T A I N S I
F Y A I S D B S S I W S P K
R E L T N E M A I L R A P N
A L I Y R L G E R M A N Y A
N L A N N I C O U N T R Y B
C A N T O N S F O N D U E S
A V E N E G N A T I O N U F
```

Solution on Page 337

ANCIENT

ASIAN

BAHT

BANGKOK

BEACH

BOXING

BUDDHIST

BURMA

CAMBODIA

CHINESE

COUNTRY

CUISINE

CULTURE

CURRY

DANCE

EXPORTS

FOOD

FOREIGN

FRIENDLY

GULF

HISTORY

HOT

ISLANDS

KINGDOM

LAOS

MALAYSIA

MEKONG

MONARCHY

MONSOONS

PACIFIC

POLITICS

RICE

SIAM

SOUTHEAST

TEMPLES

TOURISM

TRAVEL

TROPICAL

VIETNAM

WATER

Solution on Page

• Puzzles

```
P O L I T I C S A M R U B G
Y G C U I S I N E F O O D H
R N Y Q U Q A I D O B M A C
R I N H F R I E N D L Y U A
U X R I C E S R H A W L Y E
C O U N T R Y I O T T U R B
K B C F E B A S A U U R O C
D I T L C A L N R M W O T I
S L N U N N A E O A S N S F
S E E G A G M N T M D G I I
E V I Y D K S E S E N I H C
L A C I P O R T J K A E D A
P R N B O K M F U O L R D P
M T A N Z A S I A N S O U T
E H S T R O P X E G I F B O
T O U R I S M A N T E I V H
```

Solution on Page 337

ADVANCED

APPLE

BAY AREA

BUSINESS

CALIFORNIA

CHIP

CISCO

COMPANY

COMPUTER

EBAY

ENGINEERS

EXPERIMENT

FACEBOOK

GOOGLE

HIGH TECH

INDUSTRY

INNOVATORS

INTERNET

INVENTION

MICROSOFT

MONEY

PALO ALTO

PROCESSOR

RADIO

RESEARCH

SAN JOSE

SOFTWARE

STANFORD

STEVE JOBS

TECHNOLOGY

TRANSISTOR

YAHOO

Silicon Valley

```
S B I N T E R N E T X F T Y
T Y G O L O N H C E T H F Y
A E G C A L I F O R N I A N
N R B U S I N E S S E G C A
F A I I M O N E Y A M H E P
O W N Y T B O N H N I T B M
R T D A A R V G O J R E O O
D F U H P S A I B O E C O C
H O S O P M T N A S P H K O
C S T O L N O E S E X I R M
R O R L E E R E V I E P A P
A R Y V A A S R E E S H D U
E C N Z Y O C S I C J T I T
S I Y A B E L G O O G O O E
E M B N A D V A N C E D B R
R O S S E C O R P T A Q V S
```

Solution on Page 337

AMERICAN

ASSEMBLY

BRONCO

CARS

DEARBORN

DETROIT

DRIVING

EDSEL

ENGINE

ESCAPE

ESCORT

EXPLORER

FACTORY

FAIRLANE

FIESTA

FOCUS

FUSION

HISTORY

HYBRIDS

INDUSTRY

JOBS

LINCOLN

MAZDA

MERCURY

MICHIGAN

MODEL T

MOTORS

MUSTANG

NASCAR

QUALITY

TAURUS

TEMPO

TRACTORS

TRADITION

VEHICLES

WINDSTAR

Drive a Ford

```
N A S C A R A T S D N I W J
M D S E L C I H E V M B P O
O Z M O S Q U A L I T Y D B
T A U C U T R A C T O R S S
O M S N C B F H M M R O Y E
R O T O O C I S V E E T L P
S D A R F G H U E R R S B A
M E N B A Y F R N C O I M C
E L G N B D V U A U L H E S
L T S R A C I A L R P O S E
A I I N D U S T R Y X P S S
T D N O U N A C I R E M A C
S X U C R V M G A O N E F O
E E Y R O T C A F Z N T W R
I E D S E L E N G I N E R T
F U S I O N N D R I V I N G
```

Solution on Page 337

AERIAL

BRITISH

BUS

CABLE CAR

CARRIAGE

CITIES

COACH

COMMUTE

CONDUCTOR

DIESEL

DRIVER

ELECTRIC

FARE

FAST

LIGHT RAIL

LINE

LONDON

PANTOGRAPH

PASSENGERS

PUBLIC

RAILWAY

RIDE

ROUTE

STATION

STEAM

STOP

STREETS

SUBWAY

TICKET

TOUR

TRACKS

TRAFFIC

TRAINS

TRAMWAY

TRANSPORT

TRAVEL

TROLLEY

VEHICLE

WHEELS

WIRE

Trams

```
S T O P A T E K C I T T K I
R R L S E S U B W A Y O C V
E A C I R T C E L E N U O E
V V I D I E S E L P O R N H
I E F L A A G L A E I Y D I
R L F I L M O N G D T A U C
D C A G U R T A E S A W C L
W I R H T O I L N S T L T E
S L T T G R O I I B S I O N
L B O R R C A B L E C A R C
E U A A W R R N T S F R P I
E P C I T I H U S K C A R T
H T R L T C M J Z P R B R I
W E U I A M N O D N O L U E
K A S O O F A S T E E R T S
J H C C R N Y A W M A R T A
```

Solution on Page 338

AIRCRAFT

AIRPLANES

AIRPORT

APPROACH

ARRIVAL

ASPHALT

AVIATION

CEMENT

CONCRETE

DEPARTURE

DIRECTION

DISTANCE

FAA

FLAT

FLIGHTS

FLYING

GATE

GEAR

GRAVEL

JETS

LANDING

LIGHTING

LONG

MARKINGS

OVERRUN

PARALLEL

PATH

PAVEMENT

PILOTS

SAFETY

SECURITY

SKY

STRAIGHT

TAKEOFF

TARMAC

TAXIWAY

TERMINAL

TOUCHDOWN

TOWER

Runway

```
E F L I G H T S T O L I P
T A K E O F F T L A H P S A
A N O V E R R U N S T E J R
X I P Y T A V I A T I O N A
I M A L I G H T I N G A T E
W R T G J A P P R O A C H G
A E H N D I R E C T I O N L
Y T S I E R U T R A P E D E
G R A D G P U O A R M S T L
G O F N R L L U F M A E N L
N P E A A A T C T A R C E A
I R T L V N A H G C K U M R
Y I Y I E E L D N Y I R E A
L A R M L S F O O K N I V P
F R E W O T C W L S G T A R
A C D I S T A N C E S Y P K
```

Solution on Page 338

ARTISTS

ARTWORK

BOOKS

CERAMICS

CITY

CLASSICAL

COLLECTION

CULTURE

CURATOR

DISPLAY

DRAWINGS

EDUCATION

EXHIBITS

GALLERY

HISTORY

LIGHTING

LOUVRE

MODERN ART

MOMA

MONA LISA

PAINTINGS

PARIS

PASTELS

PEOPLE

PHOTOGRAPH

PICASSO

PICTURES

PRINTS

SCULPTURES

STYLE

VOLUNTEER

Art Museum Tour

```
P G N I T H G I L S I R A P
E B C N O I T A C U D E T G
L S H O P S C I M A R E C A
P M T I L I A R T I S T S L
O O B I S L E T S A P N C L
E N P S B T E C U L T U R E
P A A E H I O C A X S L X R
I L I R I P H R T M K O V Y
C I N U E M A X Y I O V U S
A S T T R A N R E D O M G E
S A I P V N V S G W B N L R
S S N L U Y E R N O I Y D U
O M G U O T K R O W T R A T
K E S C L I L C A S W O K C
Z Q N S J C U R A T O R H I
S T N I R P D I S P L A Y P
```

Solution on Page 338

ATM	MAGAZINES
BEVERAGE	MAPS
BREAD	MILK
CHIPS	MONEY
CIRCLE K	NEWSPAPERS
CLERKS	POP
COFFEE	PUMP
CONVENIENT	PURCHASE
CORNER	QUICK
CUSTOMERS	SANDWICH
DOUGHNUTS	SHOPPING
DRINKS	SLURPEES
EASY	SMALL
FAST	SNACKS
FOOD	STOP
FUEL	TOBACCO
GASOLINE	TOILETRIES
GROCERIES	WATER
GUM	
HOT DOGS	
ICE CREAM	
LOTTERY	

Convenience Store Stop

```
A T S P I H C R S M A L L B
H C E N I L O S A G X E O G
R L Z E A S E E P R U L S U
P E S A H C R U P F P O A M
M R T O N C K M S O S T N I
U K G A E F A S T P K T D L
P S N C W P P S U T N E W K
Y E I E S O S R N O I R I C
S I P G P R E E H B R Y C I
A R P A A E I M G A D E H U
E T O R P N R O U C A N O Q
E E H E R E T O C E O T D
F L S V R O C S D O R M D O
F I N E S C O U E X B P O O
O O W B C I R C L E K I G F
C T A T M A G A Z I N E S R
```

Solution on Page 338

AMSTERDAM

AQUEDUCTS

BANK

BARGES

BASIN

BOATS

BRIDGES

CARGO

CHANNELS

COMMERCE

DEEP

DITCH

ERIE CANAL

FLOW

GATES

GOODS

IRRIGATION

LAKES

LAND

LEVEL

LOCKS

MANMADE

OCEANS

PANAMA

POUND LOCK

RIVERS

ROUTE

SEA

SHIPPING

SUEZ CANAL

SUPPLY

TRANSPORT

TRAVEL

TRENCH

TUNNEL

VENICE

WATERWAYS

Down a Canal

```
W L E N N U T B H C T I D L
M P A S L A N A C E I R E A
B E A S T R A N S P O R T K
S E Q M U A B K V E N I C E
F D U P S E O B R I D G E S
L A E G D T Z B D A N A A C
O M D C Q S E C R M A T B A
W N U O V K H R A A L I Y R
C A C M K C O L D N U O P G
B M T M N O S T H A A N H O
G J S E B L E N R P M L L R
O A R R R K G K A A E E W O
O T T C O W R S R E V I R U
D S L E N N A H C E C E J T
S B N I S A B Y L N H O L E
V G N I P P I H S U P P L Y
```

Solution on Page 339

ANDROMEDA

ASTEROIDS

BIG BANG

CELESTIAL

COMETS

COSMOS

EARTH

ECLIPSE

GALAXIES

GALILEO

GASES

GRAVITY

HEAVENS

HUBBLE

JUPITER

LENS

LIGHT

MARS

MERCURY

METEORS

MILKY WAY

MOONS

NASA

NEBULAE

NEPTUNE

NIGHT

ORBITS

PHYSICS

PLANETS

RESEARCH

SATURN

SCIENCE

SKY

SPACE

STARS

STUDY

SUPERNOVA

UNIVERSE

URANUS

VENUS

Space Journey

```
S T A R S C W E C N E I C S
T H D J S N O O M A R S C T
U G C P U Y A W Y K L I M E
D I C R N P R B N A S A S N
Y N O K A E I M I Y T G A A
S E S G R E S T H G I A T L
U B M D U A S P E Q B L U P
N U O U I E V E I R R A R T
E L S M L O N O R L O X N H
V A D E M O R D N A C I N G
L E C R M E T E O R S E E I
E A O C S L D P T A E S P L
C R M U N I V E R S E P T Y
A T E R E L B B U H A C U K
P H T Y L A N H E A V E N S
S E S A G G R A V I T Y E X
```

Solution on Page 339

ACCIDENTS

ATV

BOGGING

DANGEROUS

DIRT BIKE

DRIVING

DUNE BUGGY

ENGINE

FAST

FOREST

HANDLEBARS

HELMETS

HILLS

HONDA

KAWASAKI

MOTOCROSS

MOTORCYCLE

MUDDY

POLARIS

QUAD BIKE

RACING

RECREATION

ROUGH

SAFETY

SAND

SEAT

SPEED

SPORT

STEERING

SUSPENSION

SUZUKI

TRAILS

VEHICLE

WHEELS

WILDERNESS

WOODS

YAMAHA

All-Terrain Vehicles

```
S D R I V I N G T S E R O F
T D A E L C Y C R O T O M S
Y R O N O I T A E R C E R P
S A A O G E B O G G I N G O
P Y M I W E K I B T R I D R
E T D A L I R I V T A G O T
E E U D H S L O B H A N F M
D F N I U A V D U D O E H O
J A E K T M C A E S A G S T
H S B A G N I C A R U U S O
E S U S P E N S I O N A Q C
L L G A D N O H R D F E W R
M L G W N E L C I H E V S O
E I Y A A S T E E R I N G S
T H Z K S S W H E E L S T S
S U Z U K I N P O L A R I S
```

Solution on Page 339

ANTENNA

BATTERY

BILL

CALLING

CAMERA

CHARGERS

CONNECT

COVERAGE

DATA

E-MAIL

FAMILY

FLIP

GAMES

GPS

INTERNET

IPHONE

KEYBOARD

KEYPAD

MESSAGES

MODERN

MOTOROLA

NOKIA

NUMBERS

PICTURES

PLAN

PORTABLE

RECHARGE

ROAMING

SAMSUNG

SATELLITE

SERVICE

SIGNAL

SIM CARD

SPRINT

T-MOBILE

TALK

TEXTING

TRAVEL

WIRELESS

Mobile Phone

```
E C I V R E S R E G R A H C
S M L S S K L A T A D L R O
E P E I P S G N I M A O R N
M L Y S A R E E L O T R P N
A A R E S M I L L D M O F E
G N E I L A E N E E O T A C
G I T P Q B G G T R B O M T
N C T E I I A E A N I M I A
U Q A S N C K T S R L W L R
S K B L I N T E R N E T Y E
M B I L L G A U Y O O V P M
A T E X T I N G R B P K O A
S R E B M U N A P E O I I C
K E Y P A D F G L S S A L A
I P H O N E G R A H C E R F
L E V A R T D S I M C A R D
```

Solution on Page 339

ANCIENT

ARCHES

BIG

CENOTAPH

CITIES

EVENTS

GRAVE

HISTORICAL

HONOR

ICON

IMPORTANT

LANDMARKS

LARGE

LIBERTY

LOCATION

MAUSOLEUM

MEANING

MEMORIALS

MONOLITHS

MOUNDS

NATIONAL

OBELISKS

OLD

PARTHENON

PLACE

POLITICAL

PYRAMIDS

SCULPTURE

STONEHENGE

STRUCTURE

TAJ MAHAL

TOMBS

TOWER

WASHINGTON

```
R S P O L I T I C A L T G F
E T T A J M A H A L N N S E
W N Y T R E B I L A I L C U
O E N N M T C Y T N A A U P
T V R O N O H R A N L N L Y
N E E T N L O E D P O C P R
O R G G Z M M N Y I I T A
I U R N M M A U S O L E U M
T T A I E R O Y S E N N R I
A C L H K H E N A E V T E D
C U C S F M E M O R I A L S
O R N A T I O N A L C T R V
L T M W S D N U O M I H I G
D S K S I L E B O T G T E C
J X P L A C I R O T S I H S
S C E N O T A P H T O M B S
```

ADVENTURE

AMERICAN

BUFFALO

CAMPING

CHILDREN

CHOLERA

DISEASE

EXPANSION

EXPEDITION

FAMILY

GOLD RUSH

HISTORY

HORSES

HUNTING

IDAHO

INDIANS

JOURNEY

MAP

MINERS

NEBRASKA

OREGON

OVERLAND

OXEN

PIONEERS

RAILROAD

RANCHERS

SETTLERS

SUPPLIES

TERRITORY

TRAPPERS

TRAVELERS

WESTWARD

WYOMING

On the Oregon Trail

```
H H H I S T O R Y L I M A F
U B O S R E L T T E S A N B
N U E R U T N E V D A P O N
T F X E S R E E N O I P G N
I F P N U E D R A W T S E W
N A E I R U S L R J I X R G
G L D M I D A H O I O D O N
N O I S N A P X E G T A V I
I S T R A N C H E R S O E M
P U I E S A E S I D M R R O
M P O L J O U R N E Y L L Y
A P N E R D L I H C Q I A W
C L Y V Q B X I N D I A N S
A I M A M E R I C A N R D O
N E B R A S K A R E L O H C
A S D T R A P P E R S U N M
```

Solution on Page 340

ARRIVAL

BAGGAGE

BOARDING

BUILDING

CARS

CITY

COMMUTER

DEPARTURE

ENGINEER

FOOD

FREIGHT

LATE

LINES

LOCOMOTIVE

LUGGAGE

METRO

PASSENGERS

PEOPLE

PLATFORMS

RAILROAD

RAILWAYS

ROUTE

SIGNS

STATION

STOPS

TERMINUS

TICKETS

TIMETABLE

TRACKS

TRAINS

TRANSPORT

TRAVEL

WAITING

```
E  J  P  L  A  T  F  O  R  M  S  R  A  C
M  N  L  T  R  O  P  S  N  A  R  T  U  A
E  E  G  A  G  G  U  L  B  A  E  H  X  L
T  R  A  I  N  S  G  D  O  R  G  G  R  U
R  U  L  I  N  E  S  E  A  R  N  I  O  K
O  S  W  P  H  E  J  P  R  I  E  E  U  A
K  Y  N  T  U  N  E  A  D  V  S  R  T  P
D  A  O  R  L  I  A  R  I  A  S  F  E  S
B  W  I  A  L  C  B  T  N  L  A  O  S  N
A  L  T  V  S  O  O  U  G  C  P  W  K  G
G  I  A  E  P  M  C  R  I  L  I  A  C  I
G  A  T  L  O  M  K  E  E  L  N  I  A  S
A  R  S  C  T  U  U  F  O  O  D  T  R  C
G  D  O  J  S  T  S  T  E  K  C  I  T  Y
E  L  B  A  T  E  M  I  T  Y  U  N  N  K
S  U  N  I  M  R  E  T  A  L  T  G  M  G
```

Solution on Page 340

ACCESS

ACCIDENT

ASPHALT

AUTOBAHN

BARRIER

BRIDGES

CARS

CITY

COMMUTE

CONCRETE

CROWDED

DIVIDED

DRIVERS

DRIVING

EXIT

FAST

GAS

HIGHWAY

LANES

MEDIAN

MERGE

NUMBERS

OVERPASS

PARKWAY

POLICE

RACE

RAMPS

ROADS

ROUTE

SAFER

SIGNS

SLOW LANE

TAR

TOLLS

TRAFFIC

TRAVEL

TRUCKS

TURNPIKE

UNDERPASS

VEHICLES

```
P A R E F A S D D L T S A F
H T O L L S R E E U Y I E A
V L A C C I D E N T A G A S
T M D R V W T D A I W N T K
R E S I O E E X L X K S U C
A R N R R R W Q W E R C R U
F G C C P A U T O B A H N R
F E N A I D E M L R P Y P T
I O S T L A H P S A B A I R
C S S R E B M U N F R W K A
O R A M P S S E L C I H E V
M E P S D E D I V I D G T E
M V R E I R R A B N G I U L
U I E N U P O L I C E H O S
T R V A W A C C E S S E R N
E D O L Y T I C R A C E H M
```

Solution on Page 340

ASTRONOMY

ATMOSPHERE

AXIAL TILT

CALORIS BASIN

CRATERS

DENSE

ECCENTRICITY

GAS

HEAT

HOTTEST

INNERMOST

MAGNETIC FIELD

MANTLE

MESSENGER

MOLTEN CORE

MOON

NASA

ORBITING

RED

ROCK

ROMAN GOD

ROTATION

RUPES

SATELLITE

SMALLEST PLANET

SOLAR NEBULA

SOLAR SYSTEM

SURFACE

TEMPERATURE

TERRESTRIAL

WEIRD TERRAIN

Trip to Mercury

```
T S O L A R S Y S T E M A E
T Y T I C I R T N E C C E L
E D O G N A M O R N H E A T
R E D N I N O I T A T O R N
R N E I S T L I T L A I X A
E S T A A E T S E P U R S M
S E I R B C E G R T I R O A
T L L R S A N N U S N E L T
R D L E I F C I T E N G A M
I C E T R R O T A L E N R O
A R T D O U R I R L R E N S
L A A R L S E B E A M S E P
R T S I A M S R P M O S B H
O E A E C O L O M S S E U E
C R N W H O T T E S T M L R
K S Y M O N O R T S A G A E
```

Solution on Page 341

BASEBALL

BEACHES

BIKING

BOATING

CAMPING

EVENTS

EXERCISE

FISHING

FOOTBALL

FUN

GAMBLING

GOLF

HIKING

HOBBIES

HUNTING

KNITTING

LEISURE

MOVIES

MUSIC

OUTDOORS

PARKS

PHYSICAL

PLAYING

PLEASURE

READING

RELAXING

REST

RUNNING

SAILING

SKIING

SLEEP

SOCCER

SPORTS

SURFING

SWIMMING

VACATION

Recreational Travel

```
V S K I I N G N I F R U S S
W A Q D F M O V I E S I C L
R G C G O P E S K R A P A E
E N A A O T F U N U J B M E
A I K M T L A C I S Y H P P
D K G B B I F Y T A G B I G
I I N E A L O W T E N O N N
N H I A L S I N I L I A G I
G O N C L T E N N P H T T T
N B N H S K X B G T S I J N
I B U E Q R E L A X I N G U
Y I R S P O R T S L F G O H
A E M U S I C S A I L I N G
L S W I M M I N G N I K I B
P E V E N T S R O O D T U O
Y B S O C C E R U S I E L J
```

Solution on Page 341

Solution on Page 347

Answers

Ski Resort

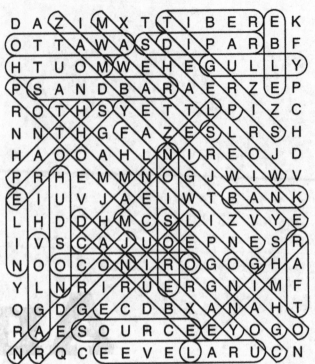

River Trip

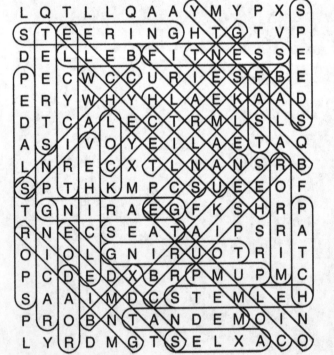

Bikes

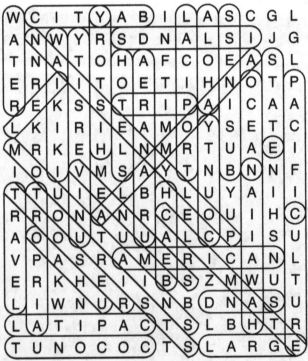

Honolulu

Nautically Speaking

Travel Forecast

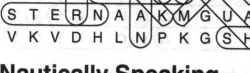

Staying at a Hotel

Transport

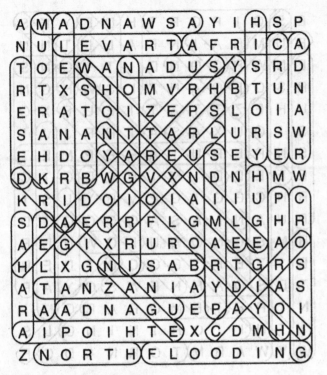

Down the Nile

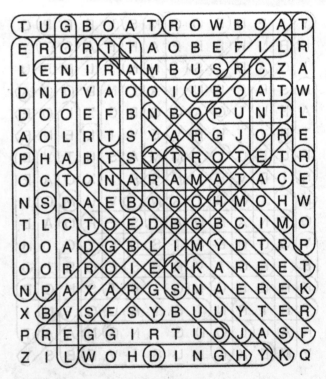

Come to Colorado

Pilgrim's Journey

All Kinds of Boats

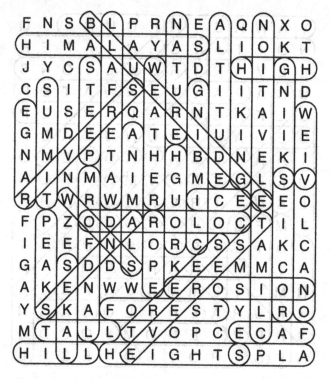

On a Mountain

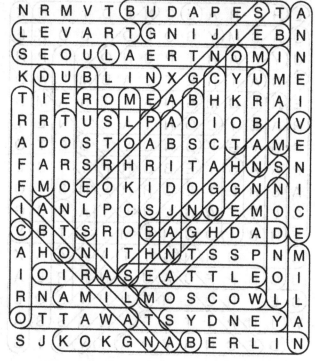

Major Cities

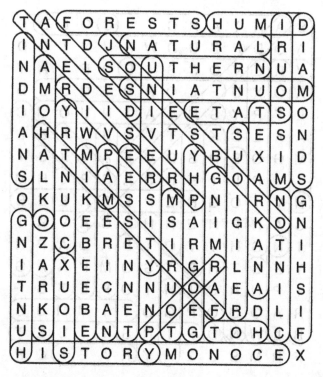

Visit Arkansas

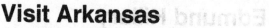

Flight

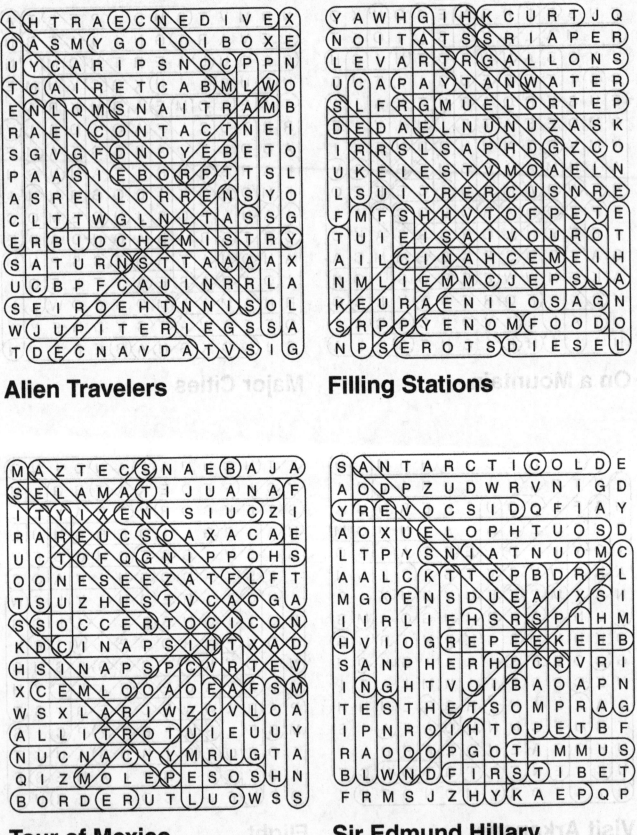

Alien Travelers

Filling Stations

Tour of Mexico

Sir Edmund Hillary

Postcards

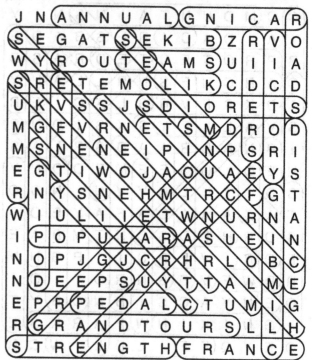
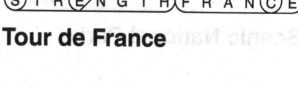

Tour de France

World's Fair

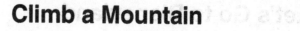

Climb a Mountain

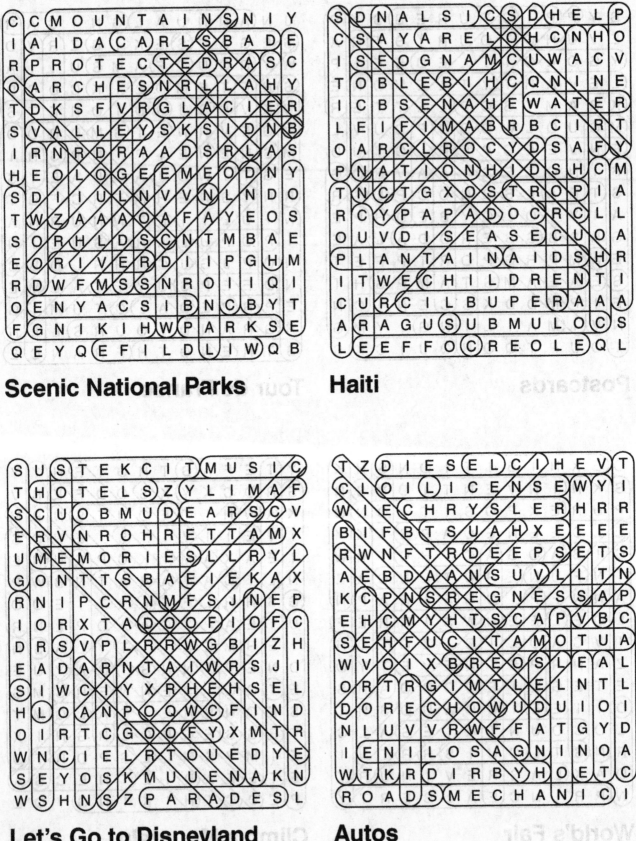

Scenic National Parks

Haiti

Let's Go to Disneyland

Autos

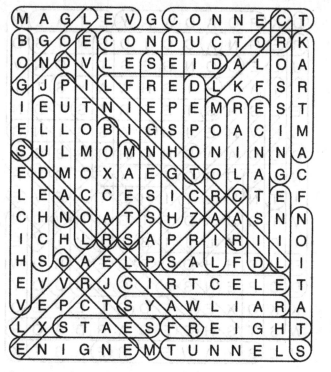

Train Travel

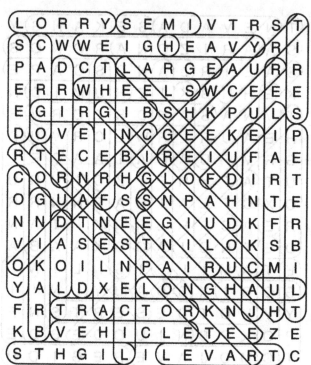

Semi Trucks

Travel Snack

Pleasure Cruise

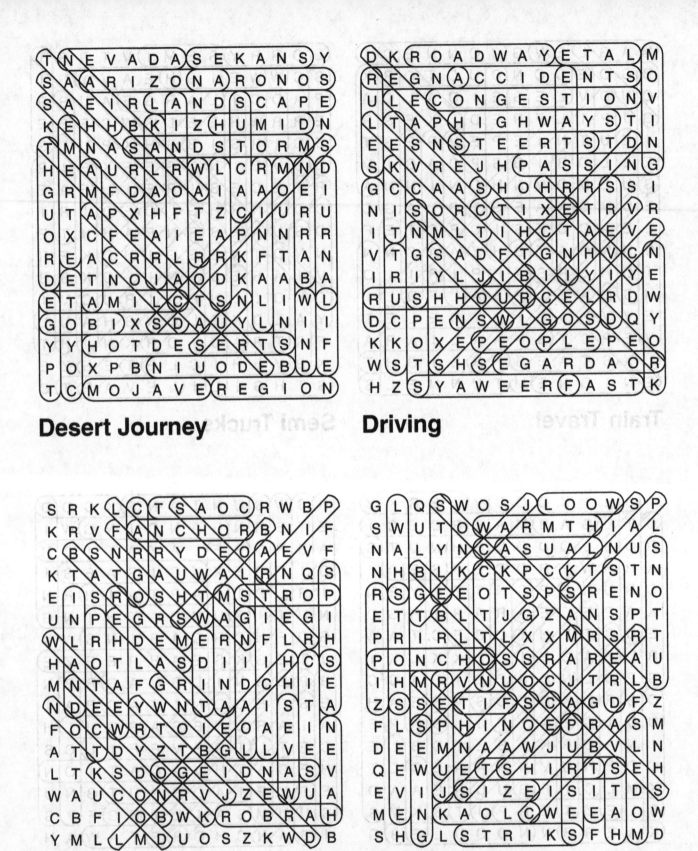

Desert Journey

Driving

Harbor

Clothes to Pack

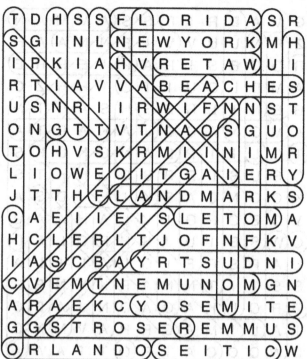

Touristy

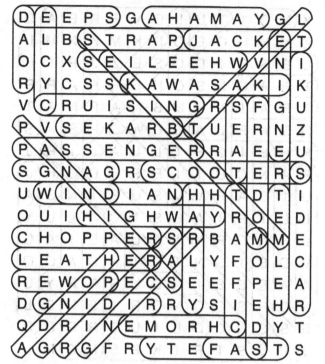

Motorcycle Touring

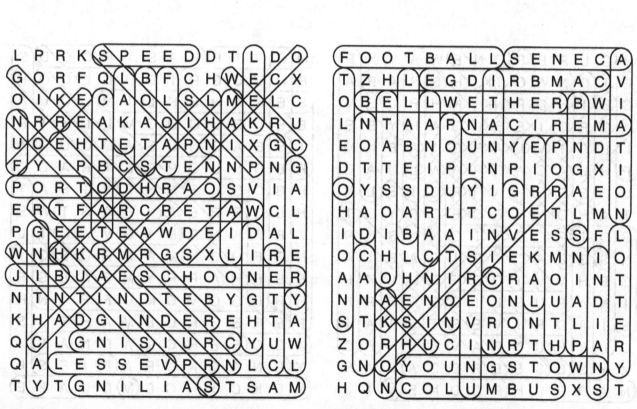

Sails Up

The Buckeye State

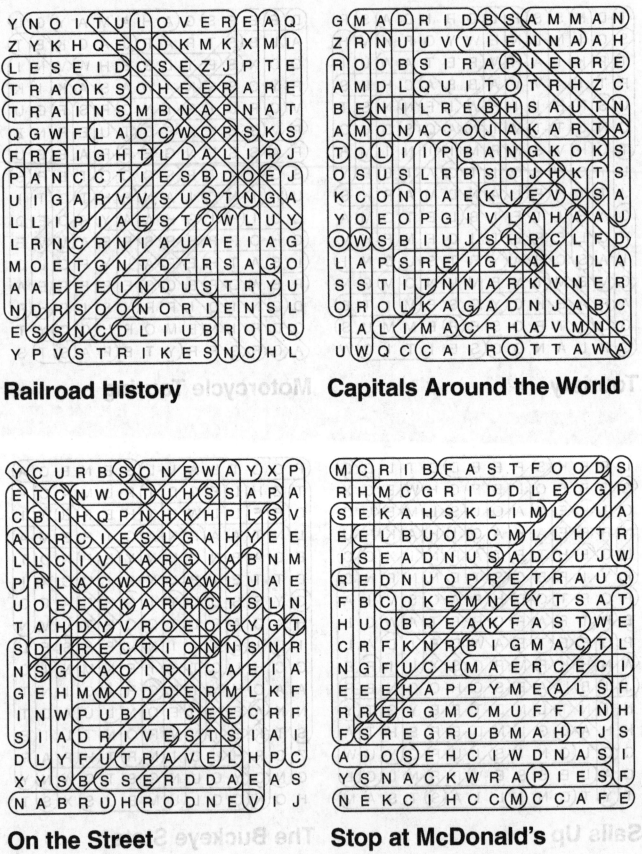

Railroad History

Capitals Around the World

On the Street

Stop at McDonald's

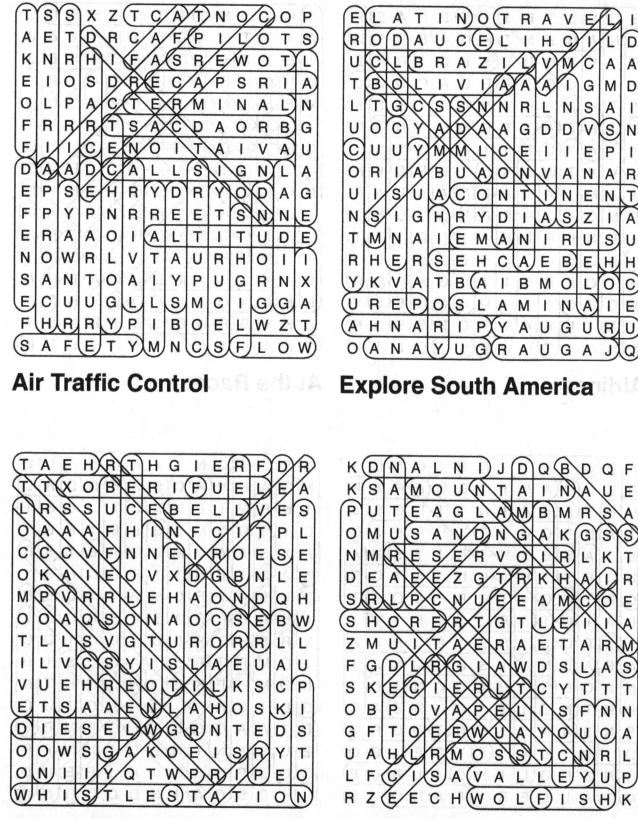

Air Traffic Control

Explore South America

Steam Train

At the Lake

Airlines

```
E U L B T E J Y T E F A S F
C N A G E N T H G I E R F U
R O V V N R G S E C I R P E
E I I Q O I F E G A G G U L
W T R P L R U N W A Y K S A
N A R F A T T E N D A N T N
I I A Y U S A I R W A Y S I
A V Y T W E S D X B E S E M
T A M I A N T E G A L E W R
P M O R I A E P N G U C H E
A E N U R L K A I G D I T A
C R O C C P C R E A E V U A
A I C E R R I T O G H R O G
B C E S A I T U B E C E S Y
I A I K F A T R O P S S A P
N N O R T H W E S T O L I P
```

Airlines

At the Races

```
S K I I N G A T S P E E D C
W I T T R A C K G P H V B J
I E X X E Y G Y H O R S E J
M D G H C L L N L K A I P M
M F N L N L I Y I M U Q N O
I O I U A Q M B A W T C D T
N N T R O P S R O T O M Y O
G F A O I H A L Y M Y R V C
N O K C R T Y D E A W N L R
I I S Z H C Y E L D U O A O
N T A O B B Y E R Q D C N S
N R N M R D R C B G K O M S
U A X E C A M E L C A E G A
R K D A O R F F O E V R S P
C K V B R U O T B I R X D V
G N I L I A S B I C Y C L E
```

At the Races

Going to Museums

```
E B C I F I T N E I C S O X
R E U C A N T I Q U E R A R
U N T A P A I N T I N G S J
T A B S C U L P T U R E S G
L U A E E X H I B I T S U A
U R R S S H V C U R A T O R
C A T N O I T C E L L O C T
D L I D T S R O T I S I V I
V E F C L T R E A S U R E S
N A A D N O I S S I M D A T
R R C E S R U A S O N I D I
E N T N O I T A C U D E A C
D S A N C I E N T O U R S
D I S P L A Y S T C E J B O
O N E R D L I H C I L B U P
M G A L L E R Y F A M O U S
```

Going to Museums

Motel Pool

```
G F L J G N I T A O L F L E
N G A K N R C S R E D D A L
I N P M I E H K O X L E N I
D I S D N M E S L E I P E T
A X S E A M M W O R E T S R
W A B T E U I I P C N H E Y
D L S A L S C M R I C L C L
I E R E C R A S E R O H O I
V R E H E K L U T E O I O U
I O M P T R S I A C L S T N
N M H E K E T W D H K I U G
G D S R N I T R A C I U B E
D T W A C O D E L O P M B E
E U S L N T N L D I K M F P
C O J P O E O J K J F E U D
K I D S C W I N D O O R N P
```

Motel Pool

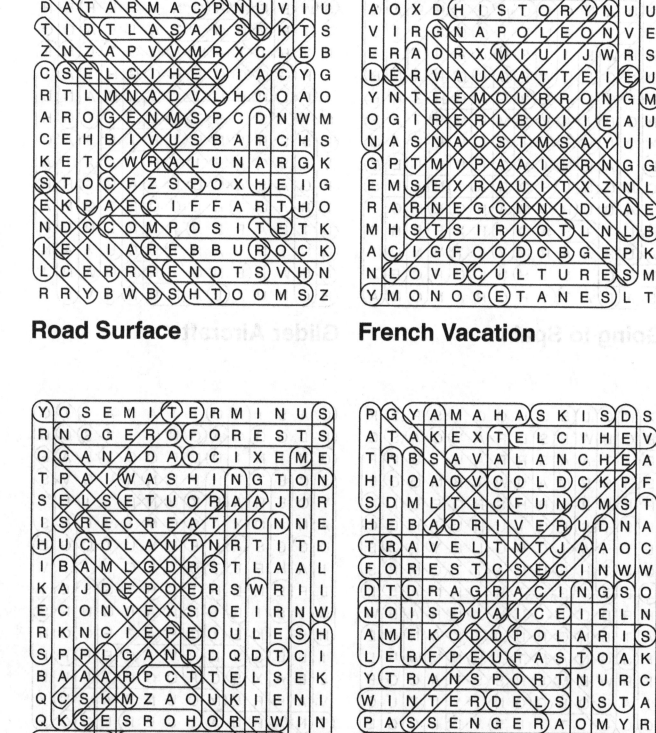

Road Surface

French Vacation

Pacific Crest Trail

Snowmobile

Going to Spain

```
K I N G D O M C U L T U R E
S Y R T N U O C U I A D L U
R D A N C E C H O I P R A Q
E A T L A N T I C C S X T I A
R H W E J I S N L A N I I A
O N C L Q W E D P O P A N B
L F O L I L B E A C H Z R E
P O B I A V N M E M S T A F
X L V T I I O L U E F A G
E O T A E N I M C L S E L E C
C B G S L S D R A I N A P S
I A U U R O M A N C E M O I
R L T T S A O C R X R E R B
A L R W A R M Y L T Y N U I
Y R O T S I H U K C P C E Z
S A P A T Y H C R A N O M A
```

Going to Spain

Glider Aircraft

```
R T F A R C R I A X A J Y J
B M I L I T A R Y Q Y F B S
S W B E T R G N I Y L F B H
Z T E V N O I T A I V A O Q
P X R I T A W A G G T L H E
L R G O G G L H G G H I A T
I P L N P H T P D N G A N U
M I A S I S T E L O I T G H
P S S R L D R T F I L S A C
V L S G A E I I H T A X R A
K O A S W G D L A A R G P R
L R A O S R L O G E T L A P
D T P A P E R I M R L N A N
G N I N I A R T D C U I A J
U O W F E N G I N E Q W N J
H C N U A L A N D R R V E T
```

Glider Aircraft

Suburbs

```
X H O L S C H O O L S P S K
B C U W F S D R A Y O A S G
P I T A A S R R A U I E P F
E R K P I R H S R O P U L N
R F S I S L G I U H U I H E C
F S T R W I D B O L E Y P O E
E T E T H E U U A T T O M P S
C R D C I I U N X U R A B W
T A T B N O R U O T K W N O E
R F S G N A M T I H N M W R L
A F R W B M L N S S P A O O P
F I A D O B G G N I Y L T U O
F C C C I T I E S V D L C G E
Z O N I N G T R E E S I H P
```

Suburbs

Resort

```
C A S I N O I T A C A V I G
F L O G O A G N I I K S C U
G N I N I D M P O O L L A E
S C B T T H F E N A U C V S
Y O E R A E K U N B T I L T
A N A O X A S D M I S E N S
D C C S A L E E V U T O G E
I A H E L T D I L O I I V V
L R E R E H T C H T S S E I
O B S I R I N R A P G H O S
H I K E I O E A Z F O O N
I B S S E R V I C E P F E
S E A X S C F O O D T P P P
V A R R E M O U N T A I N X
T N A R U A T S E R L N O E
I B P N S W I M M I N G L N
```

Resort

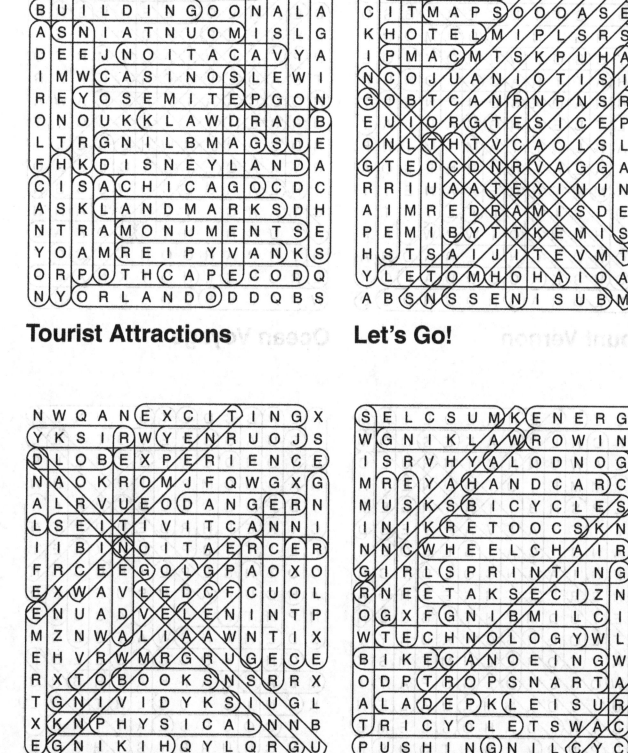

Tourist Attractions

Let's Go!

Adventure Travel

Human Powered

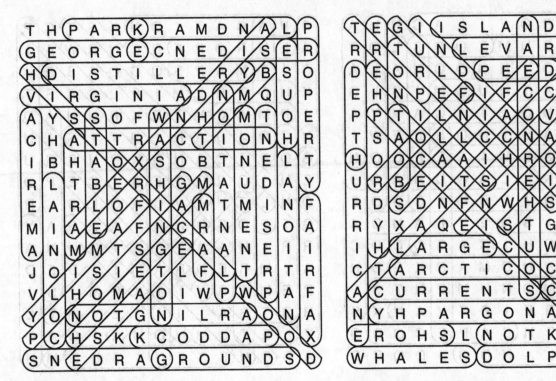

Mount Vernon

Ocean Voyage

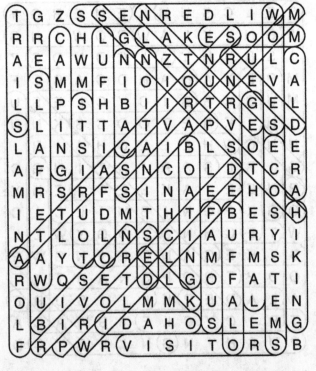

Yellowstone National Park

Stop for a Bite

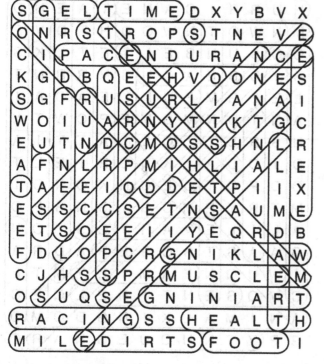

Run Away

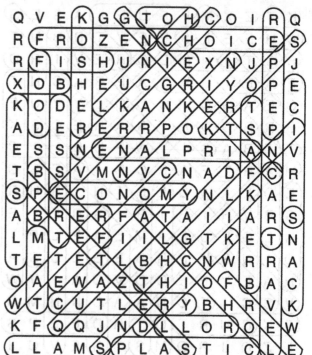

Airline Meals

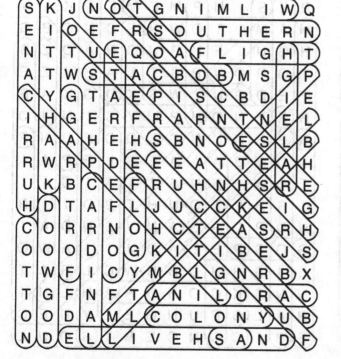

North Carolina

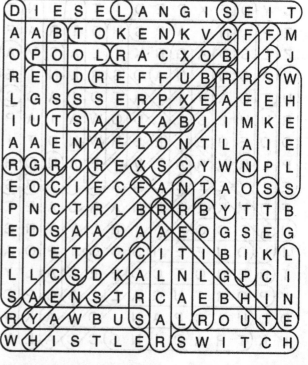

Railroad Words

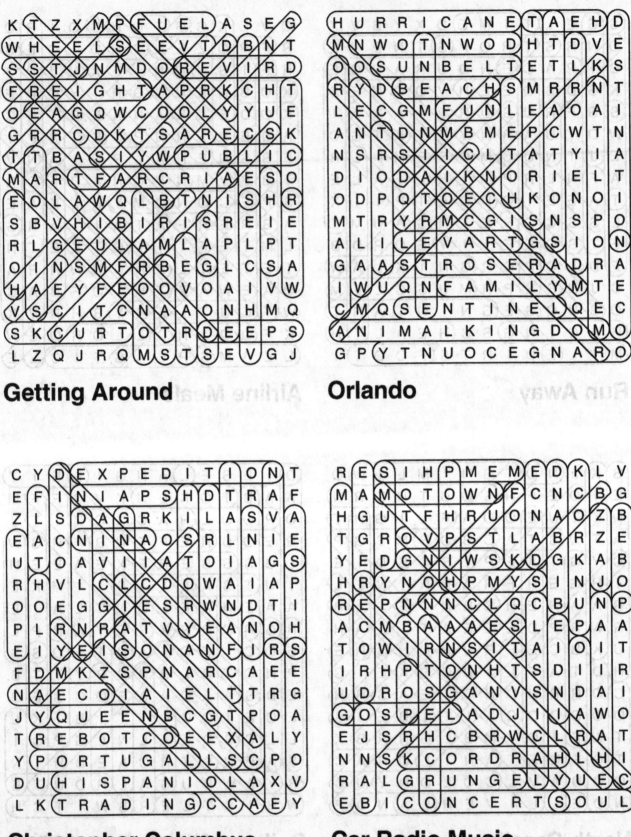

Getting Around

Orlando

Christopher Columbus

Car Radio Music

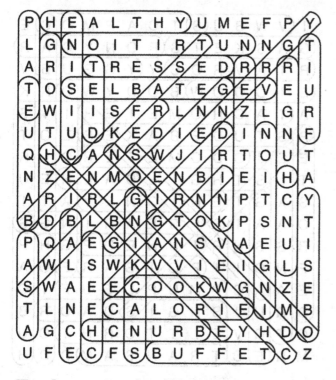

Eating on the Road

Kennedy Space Center

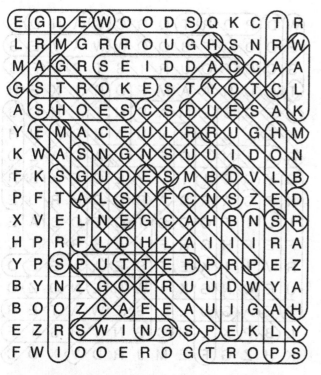

Golf Vacation

Courier

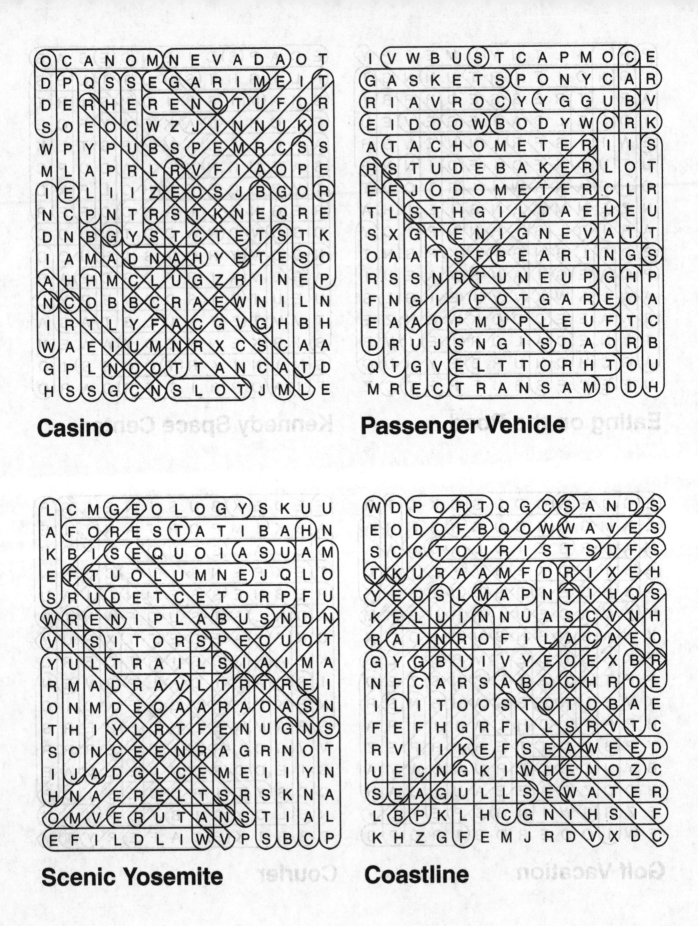

Casino

Passenger Vehicle

Scenic Yosemite

Coastline

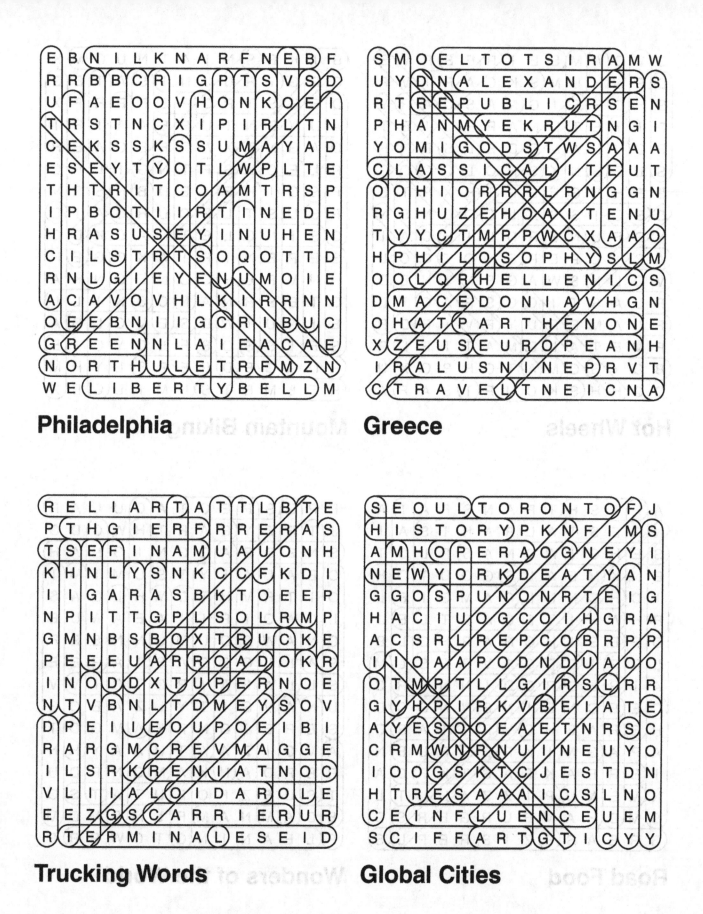

Philadelphia

Greece

Trucking Words

Global Cities

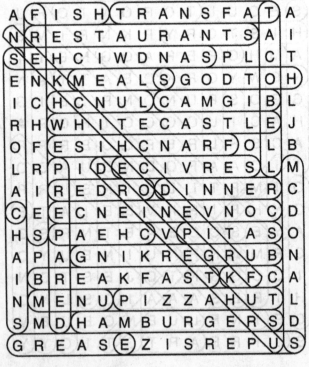

Hot Wheels

Mountain Biking

Road Food

Wonders of the World

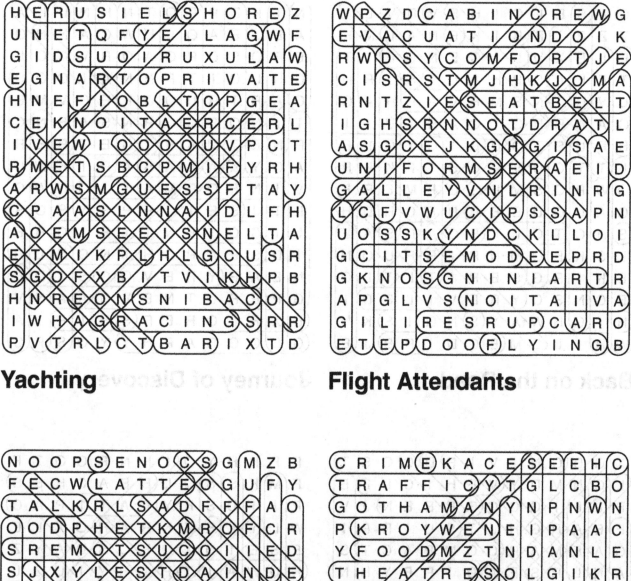

Yachting

Flight Attendants

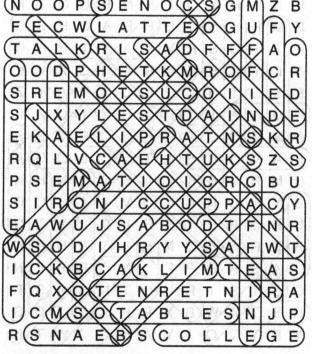

Coffee Stop

Gotham

Back on the Road

```
C W S E L C I H E V D V L I
V Z P I B B I K E N A L M K
E L E X U L I C E N S E T T
T E E A S P H A L T S T R H
U V D T N E M E V A P R A G
O A W R R O T C A R T U I I
R R U S I O D B I C Y C L E
L T T C D V P O B I F K E R
O W R O S M E S O F M E R F
G A U O D E B R N F G R D H
S H C T O L L R O A D S A E
L S K E O M N R I R R U O N
E K I R G S E R I T L T L G
E C N S O Y R E V I L E D I
H I G H W A Y S N G I S K N
W R I L C M E G D I R B J E
```

Journey of Discovery

```
N T K D P P O T N H N U K A
A E J E A O L U W C A N N O
E R O S C R O A O R V C O L
C R U O I T P N N A I O O S
O A R T R U O O K E G V M E
T I N O E G C R N S A E N C
R N E T M A R T U E T R E R
A O Y K A L A S A R I K W U
V I N F O R M A T I O N N O
E T J S E I C E P S N S O S
L I S C I E N T I F I C R E
I D S E A R C H I N G N L R
N E A P Y R E V O C S I D E
G P E R U T N E V D A A N V
E X P L O R E R S H I P I A
G E O G R A P H Y Y Q S F C
```

Electric Cars

```
X G B G N I V I R D C O S T
L C N M D Y V E H I C L E E
P L F I G C C G R E E N J V
E E A R G H J T S U I R P I
G A E M A R C O M P A C T S
A N L R S E A D I R B Y H N
E Y G O L O N H C E T I K E
L E P E E F F I C I E N T P
I E L I B O M O T U A O A X
M P U B Q S N O I S S I M E
U O G U A O A Y R E T T A B
I W I Q M W Q G F U T U R E
H E N I G N E G N A R L O T
T R C S A V I N G S O L T L
I A W O L S L E E H W O O V
L C A Y L D N E I R F P M V
```

Dubai

```
F F H H Y O I K N P G O T F
F M K S S Q L B E A C H E S
P I I U S K Y L A T I P A C
W L Y L E Z K R A H O X L E
E S E T N X O K C S D A Y Z
K U W A I T P I H Y I U Z L
W M Z N S C R E H C P V B S
F A M O U S I T N D L O G A
U M R V B K L A R S D N H N
B Y H C R A N O M I I S O D
U P O F E I G E L D V V T L
R Z R W F O N L L T E H E U
J A S H O P P I N G R E L N
O S T S I R U O T N S A S E
R E T A W B X R H A E T D S
Y R Y V Q I V W H O J W T E
```

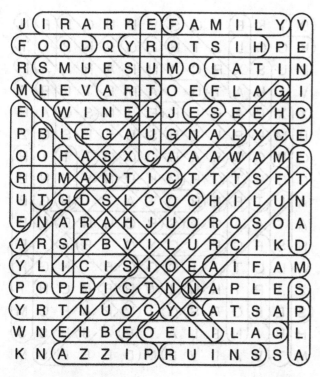

```
G I S L A N D R A W D E C E        H L R I G W O C A T T L E C
D V E Y T N E M A I L R A P        H T G I B L U B B O C K H S
D R M C R I C K E T I N M O        N S R G O E G E L L O C N D
D I A N A O L C O E V K B R        O A D O A G L L A B T O O F
N T H U U S T N H F E I R U        T O M Y W L R I S O R T S A
U O T N G T J S M I R N I E        T C O U T T V A O J D S H R
O U T I Y O C I I S P G D P        O F E S E I R E N I F E R M
P R E O H N I A R H O S G I        C L G L A L S O S D A V I N
Y I C N C E H A S E O L E N        H U O O D P O R F T E I N G
B S A J R H B E A T L E S T        K G M N R N L R E V O L C H
G M L A A E S C G A L A N G        A M A G E O A E T V C N H T
U C A C N A O B U P E N W          U E L H D S D H G E I I E U
R I P K O G T T C B C H S D        S X A O R A T E N R P N S O
E R I P M E O E H C R U H C        T I E R O I J A O A A C U S
D N A L T O C S A S E L A W        I C H N B S P U R S P L A S
J A O X F O R D N W O R C T        N O T S U O H D E S E R T W
```

English Holiday   **The Lone Star State**

```
J I R A R R E F A M I L Y V        S H A R E M A R F D J D F V
F O O D Q Y R O T S I H P E        L C O L O R S K I O E A R T
R S M U E S U M O L A T I N        I R A C B M E G K V C P P S
M L E V A R T O E F L A G I        D R E P B U I T E E T U O T
E I W I N E L J E S E E H C        E E V P E T M L U I N Z S I
P B L E G A U G N A L X C E        L C I M A R O N A P E M I L
O O F A S X C A A A W A M E        E O T L U P T R G S M O N G
R O M A N T I C T T T S F T        N R A I T K T U E C U O R E
U T G D S L C O C H I L U N        S D G F Y R J R R U C R C D
E N A R A H J U O R O S O A        O I E Q O R U Y U E O K A O
A R S T B V I L U R C I K D        P M N P O T R U S N D R P M
Y L I C I S I O E A I F A M        F A I S C O T L O A Y A T E
P O P E I C T N N A P L E S        L G N I T N I R P T R D U N
Y R T N U O C Y C A T S A P        A E P S E G V A X U O B R E
W N E H B E O E L I L A G L        S S I V H C A M E R A H E C
K N A Z Z I P R U I N S S A        H H E T Q E L P O E P L P S
```

Italian Tour   **Take Pictures**

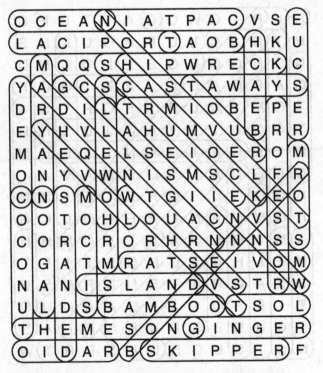

Stuck on Gilligan's Island

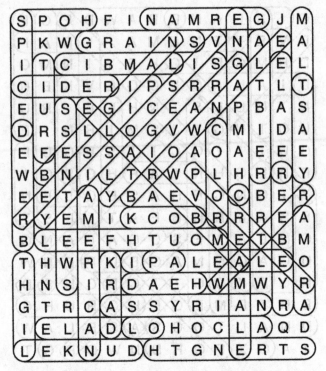

Beers Around the World

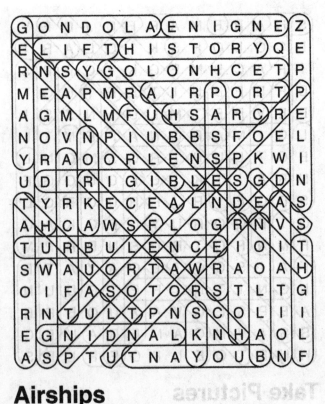

Airships

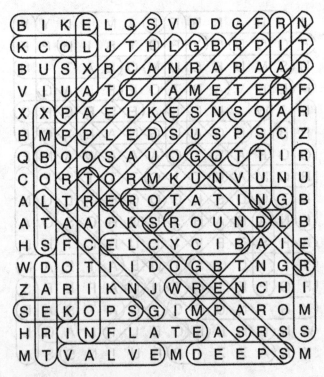

Bicycle Wheels

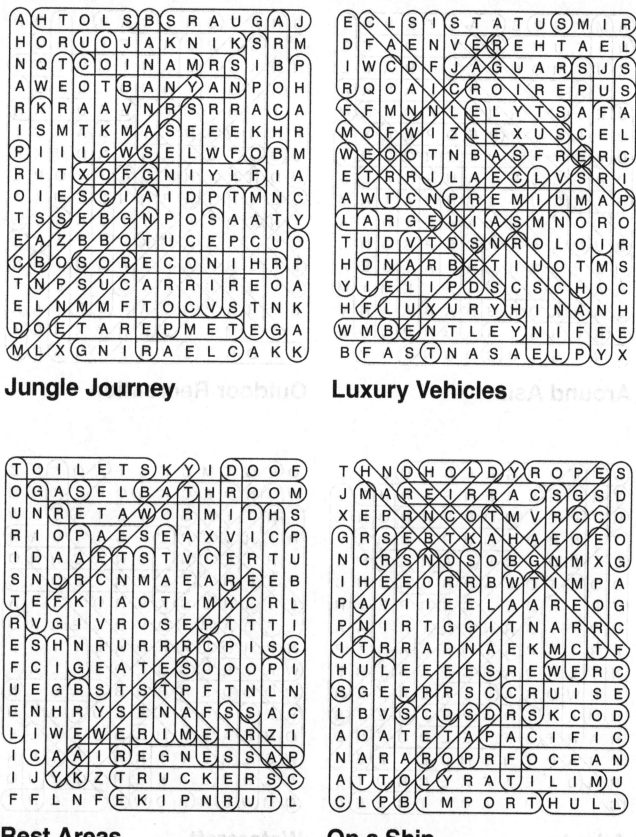

Jungle Journey

Luxury Vehicles

Rest Areas

On a Ship

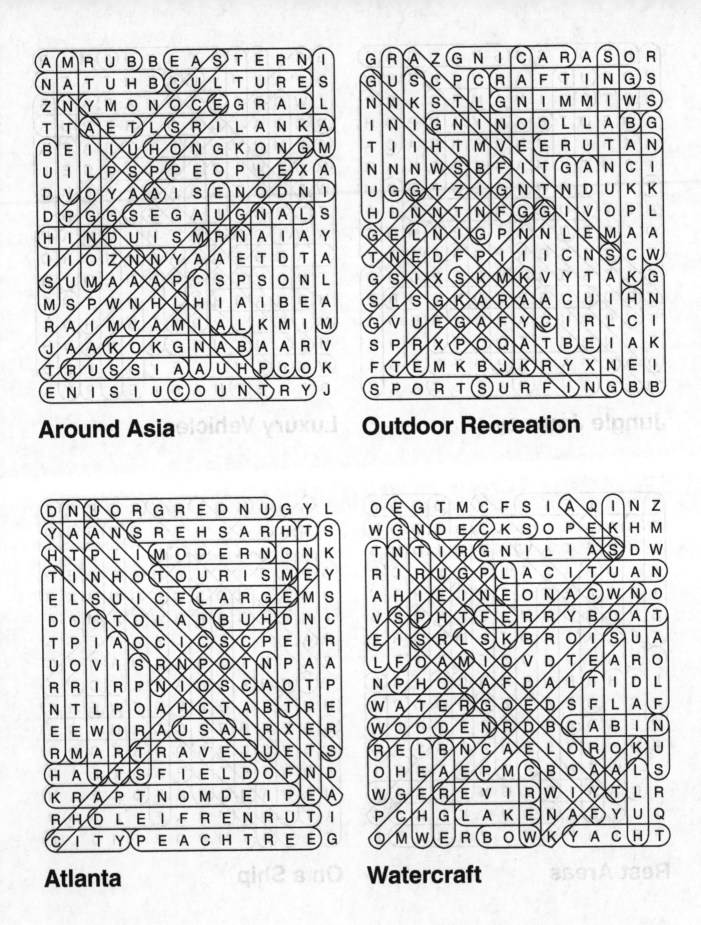

Around Asia

Outdoor Recreation

Atlanta

Watercraft

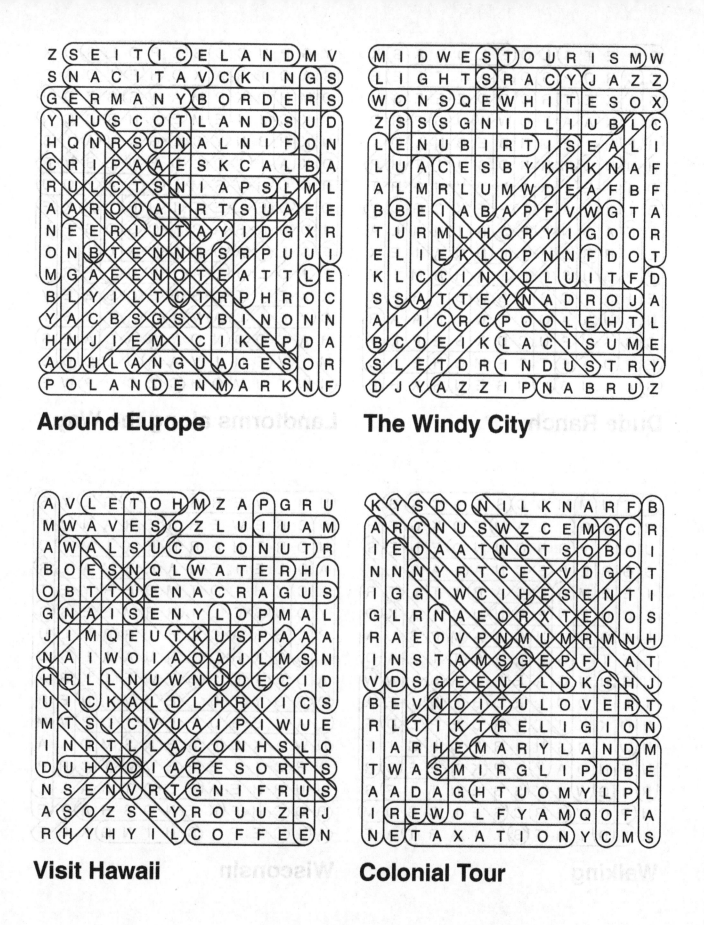

Around Europe

The Windy City

Visit Hawaii

Colonial Tour

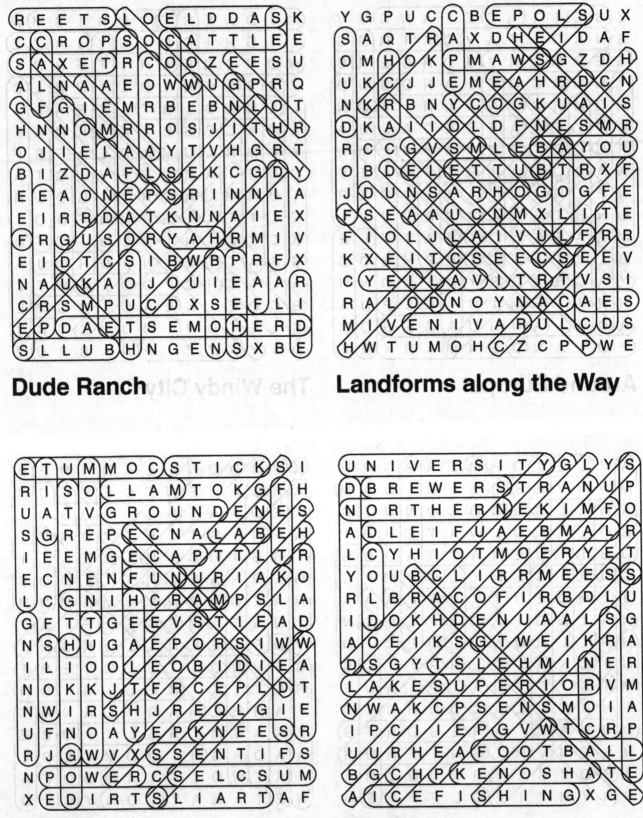

Dude Ranch

Landforms along the Way

Walking

Wisconsin

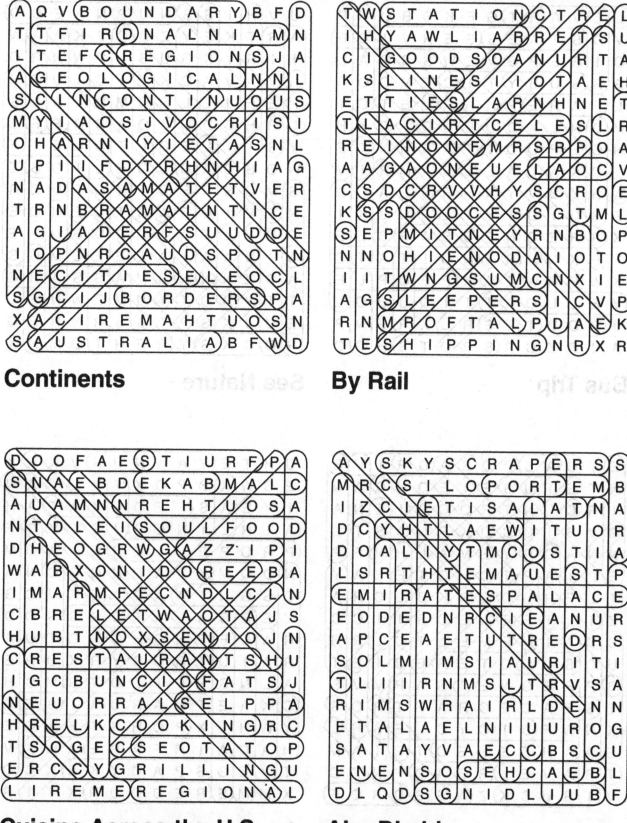

Continents

By Rail

Cuisine Across the U.S.

Abu Dhabi

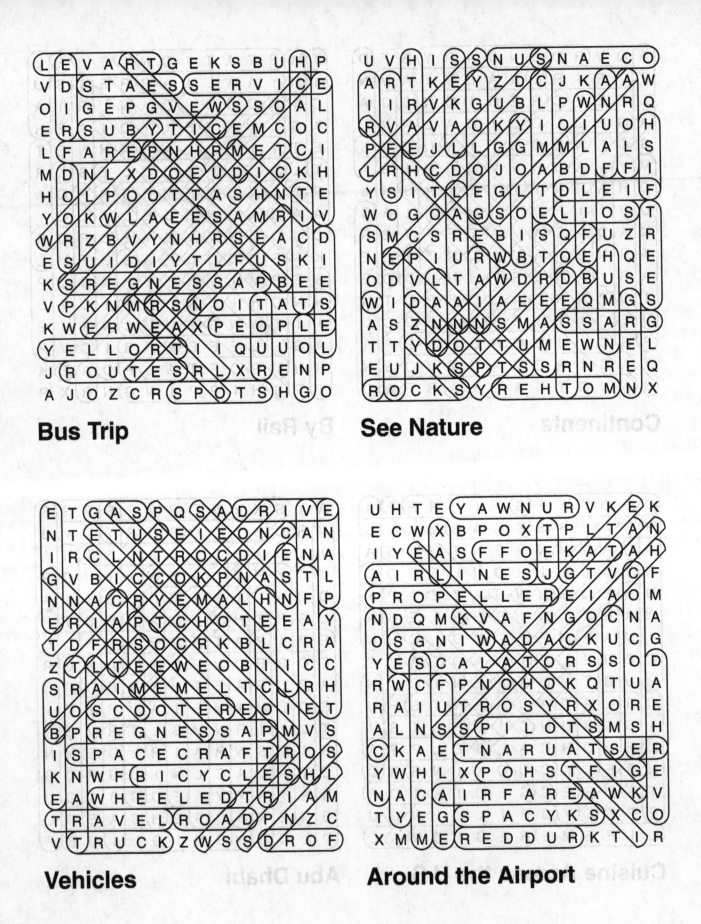

Bus Trip

See Nature

Vehicles

Around the Airport

Switzerland

Thailand

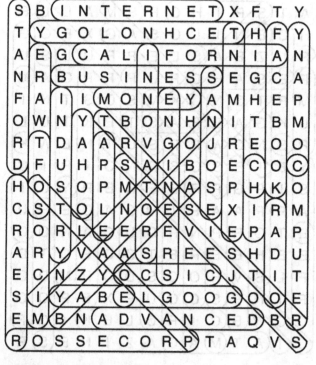

Silicon Valley

Drive a Ford

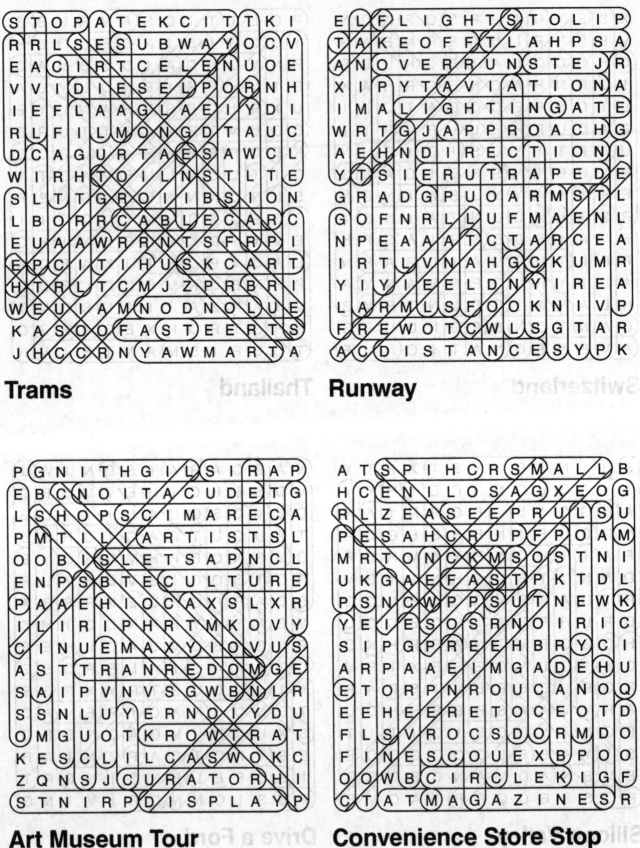

Trams

Runway

Art Museum Tour

Convenience Store Stop

Down a Canal

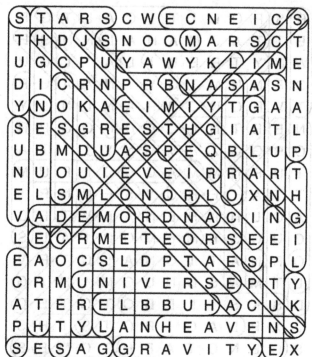

Space Journey

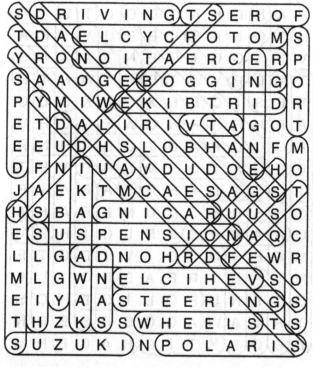

All-Terrain Vehicles

Mobile Phone

R	S	P	O	L	I	T	I	C	A	L	T	G	F
E	T	T	A	J	M	A	H	A	L	N	N	S	E
W	N	Y	T	R	E	B	I	L	A	I	L	C	U
O	E	N	N	M	T	C	Y	T	N	A	A	U	P
T	V	R	O	N	O	H	R	A	N	L	N	L	Y
N	E	E	T	N	L	O	E	D	P	O	C	P	R
O	R	G	G	Z	P	M	M	N	Y	I	I	T	A
I	U	R	N	M	M	A	U	S	O	L	E	U	M
T	T	A	I	E	R	O	Y	S	E	N	N	R	I
A	C	L	H	K	H	E	N	A	E	V	T	E	D
C	U	C	S	F	M	E	M	O	R	I	A	L	S
O	R	N	A	T	I	O	N	A	L	C	T	R	V
L	T	M	W	S	D	N	U	O	M	I	H	I	G
D	S	K	S	I	L	E	B	O	T	G	T	E	C
J	X	P	L	A	C	I	R	O	T	S	I	H	S
S	C	E	N	O	T	A	P	H	T	O	M	B	S

Monuments

H	H	H	I	S	T	O	R	Y	L	I	M	A	F
U	B	O	S	R	E	L	T	T	E	S	A	N	B
N	U	E	R	U	T	N	E	V	D	A	P	O	N
T	F	X	E	S	R	E	E	N	O	I	P	G	N
I	F	P	N	U	E	D	R	A	W	T	S	E	W
N	A	E	I	R	U	S	L	R	J	I	X	R	G
G	L	D	M	I	D	A	H	O	I	O	D	O	N
N	O	I	S	N	A	P	X	E	G	T	A	V	I
I	S	T	R	A	N	C	H	E	R	S	O	E	M
P	U	I	E	S	A	E	S	I	D	M	R	R	O
M	P	O	L	J	O	U	R	N	E	Y	L	L	Y
A	P	N	E	R	D	L	I	H	C	Q	I	A	W
C	L	Y	V	Q	B	X	I	N	D	I	A	N	S
A	I	M	A	M	E	R	I	C	A	N	R	D	O
N	E	B	R	A	S	K	A	R	E	L	O	H	C
A	S	D	T	R	A	P	P	E	R	S	U	N	M

On the Oregon Trail

E	J	P	L	A	T	F	O	R	M	S	R	A	C
M	N	L	T	R	O	P	S	N	A	R	T	U	A
E	E	G	A	G	G	U	L	B	A	E	H	X	L
T	R	A	I	N	S	G	D	O	R	G	G	R	U
R	U	L	I	N	E	S	E	A	R	N	I	O	K
O	S	W	P	H	E	J	P	R	I	E	E	U	A
K	Y	N	T	U	N	E	A	D	V	S	R	T	P
D	A	O	R	L	I	A	R	I	A	S	F	E	S
B	W	I	A	L	C	B	T	N	L	A	O	S	N
A	L	T	V	S	O	O	U	G	C	P	W	K	G
G	I	A	E	P	M	C	R	I	L	I	A	C	I
G	A	T	L	O	M	K	E	E	L	N	I	A	S
A	R	S	C	T	U	U	F	O	O	D	T	R	C
G	D	O	J	S	T	S	T	E	K	C	I	T	Y
E	L	B	A	T	E	M	I	T	Y	U	N	N	K
S	U	N	I	M	R	E	T	A	L	T	G	M	G

Train Stations

P	A	R	E	F	A	S	D	D	L	T	S	A	F
H	T	O	L	L	S	R	E	E	U	Y	I	E	A
V	L	A	C	C	I	D	E	N	T	A	G	A	S
T	M	D	R	V	W	T	D	A	I	W	N	T	K
R	E	S	I	O	E	E	X	L	X	K	S	U	C
A	R	N	R	R	R	W	Q	W	E	R	C	R	U
F	G	C	C	P	A	U	T	O	B	A	H	N	R
F	E	N	A	I	D	E	M	L	R	P	Y	P	T
I	O	S	T	L	A	H	P	S	A	B	A	I	R
C	S	S	R	E	B	M	U	N	F	R	W	K	A
O	R	A	M	P	S	S	E	L	C	I	H	E	V
M	E	P	S	D	E	D	I	V	I	D	G	T	E
M	V	R	E	I	R	R	A	B	N	G	I	U	L
U	I	E	N	U	P	O	L	I	C	E	H	O	S
T	R	V	A	W	A	C	C	E	S	S	E	R	N
E	D	O	L	Y	T	I	C	R	A	C	E	H	M

Highways

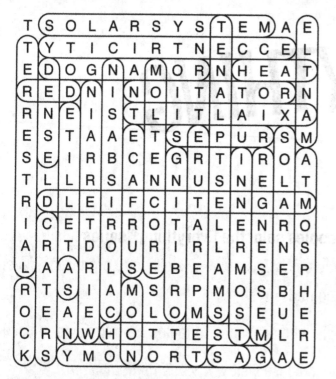

Trip to Mercury

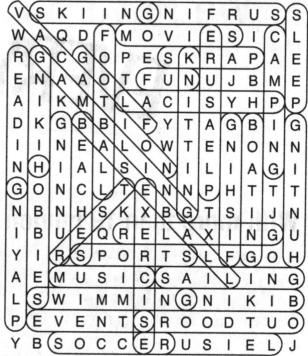

Recreational Travel

We Have EVERYTHING® on Anything!

With more than 19 million copies sold, the Everything® series has become one of America's favorite resources for solving problems, learning new skills, and organizing lives. Our brand is not only recognizable—it's also welcomed.

The series is a hand-in-hand partner for people who are ready to tackle new subjects—like you!

For more information on the Everything® series, please visit *www.adamsmedia.com*.

The Everything® list spans a wide range of subjects, with more than 500 titles covering 25 different categories:

Business	History	Reference
Careers	Home Improvement	Religion
Children's Storybooks	Everything Kids	Self-Help
Computers	Languages	Sports & Fitness
Cooking	Music	Travel
Crafts and Hobbies	New Age	Wedding
Education/Schools	Parenting	Writing
Games and Puzzles	Personal Finance	
Health	Pets